D0734605

LUTHERAN
BOOK
OF
PRAYER

CONCORDIA PUBLISHING HOUSE · SAINT LOUIS

9 780570 030058

Concordia Publishing House, St. Louis, Missouri
© 1970 Concordia Publishing House
Library of Congress Catalog Card No. 76-119916

MANUFACTURED IN THE UNITED STATES OF AMERICA

26 27 28 29 30   05 04 03

CONTENTS

6. Prayers for Others

9

PREFACE

Lutheran Book of Prayer is issued in the conviction that the prayer of a Christian is not some futile gesture, purely pious exercise, or vain escape mechanism from reality, but the divinely ordained means by which a child of God taps that limitless reservoir of power which the Almighty has placed at the disposal of those who come and ask in the name of Jesus. The Lord's gracious invitation "Call upon Me in the day of trouble; I will deliver thee, and thou shalt glorify Me" (Ps. 50:15) is only one of the many Scriptural authentications for the preparation of this volume.

Needless to say, this collection of prayers is offered not with the purpose of stereotyping the petitions and praises which the loyal disciple formulates when he appears before his God. Instead, it is intended to assist, encourage, and stimulate the Christian in his life of communion with the heavenly Father. As he engages in personal or corporate prayer, the believer not infrequently experiences difficulty in accurately expressing his needs and desires. For such moments this volume can be a convenient resource book of thoughts, words, and phrases with which to articulate the inmost longings of the human heart.

Furthermore, this new edition of *Lutheran Book of Prayer* presents a much broader range of prayer topics than its predecessor by the same name and it seeks to respond to the unique needs of modern Christian life with fresh prayer forms, patterns of thought, and language. Contributors to this booklet, in addition to the general editor, include Dr. William Buege, Pastors Harry N. Huxhold and Richard C. Stuckmeyer, and Mrs. Robert Springsteen. Our collective hope is that all who see these prayers will experience the fulfillment of the Savior's promise, "Ask, and it will be given you; seek, and you will find; knock, and it will be opened to you." (Matt. 7:7)

J. W. ACKER, D. D.
General Editor

PRAYERS
FOR
MORNING AND EVENING

Sunday Morning

Lord God, heavenly Father, who on this day began Your work of creation, today make and keep us the new creation of Your fatherly love through Your Word.

Lord Jesus, who on this day conquered death and rose from the grave, help us today to die to sin and to rise to new life with You.

O Holy Spirit, who on this day came upon our Lord's disciples with power, come to us today with power to give us a victorious faith and humble obedience.

O blessed Trinity, who cannot be contained in houses of worship made with men's hands, make Your presence felt among us today as we worship You in Your sanctuary. Bless those who speak and teach in Your name and us who hear and meditate on Your Word. Accept our hymns of praise, and hear our prayers for forgiveness. Sustain the new life You gave us in Holy Baptism, and nourish our faith as we feed on our Lord's body and blood. Help us as Your faithful children to translate Your Word into a life of selfless service. For Jesus' sake. Amen.

Sunday Evening

Gracious God, as we come to the close of this holy day of worship and rest, we pause once more to lift our hearts in adoration and thanksgiving to Your throne. You touched the lips of the pastor with glowing coals from Your altar, and by the power of Your Holy Spirit Your Word truly moved our hearts. The message of Your love in Christ revived our spirits and filled us with desire to live for Him who died for us.

We confess to You that we have blundered, but You have corrected. We have stumbled; You have lifted up. We have sinned; You have pardoned. Accept our praise for Your undeserved mercies.

Give us grace and strength to bear the burdens of the week ahead, resist its temptations, shoulder its responsibilities, and seize its opportunities. In all our experiences lead us by Your mighty hand, and make clear Your will for us in all our choices and plans. As we now entrust ourselves to Your protecting arms, grant us restful sleep tonight and refreshment and strength tomorrow to serve You and our fellowmen; through Christ, our Lord. Amen.

Monday Morning

At the beginning of another day we come before You, O Lord, with grateful hearts for Your protection during this past night and for the privilege of seeing the light of this new day. As we begin another week of activity, we ask You to be with us. Give us wisdom and strength for the tasks which await us. Help us to perform our duties faithfully and to find that joy which comes from seeking You in all we do.

Although we live in the world, preserve us from being of the world. In all our associations make us considerate and friendly. In successes keep us humble, in disappointments patient. In temptations shield us, in danger protect us, and in sorrow comfort us.

Mindful that we are Your children through Christ and members of His body, we thank You for our spiritual heritage in the church. Extend Your church through us wherever we go, so that all who behold our Christian lives may be moved to accept Jesus as their personal Redeemer also. In His name we pray. Amen.

Monday Evening

As the shadows of night gather about us, dear heavenly Father, Your love dispels the darkness and fills our lives with the radiance of divine assurance and satisfying peace. Each moment of this day has been a gift of Your grace. Each breath has been a token of Your sustaining power. Forgive us where we have been selfish, forgetful, or ungrateful. Grant us Your favor also this night.

At the close of this day we remember in our prayers the sick, the afflicted, the troubled and distressed, and all who need Your help and support. You know the weaknesses as well as the needs and wants of Your children everywhere. Comfort and strengthen them, O Father, according to Your wisdom and will. Give them the certainty of Your constant concern and protection.

Help us to rest tonight secure in the embrace of Your everlasting arms. Through refreshing sleep grant us renewed energy for another day of service. And tomorrow give us courage and confidence to walk whatever road Your fatherly love may choose for us. In Jesus' name. Amen.

Tuesday Morning

Gracious God, by whose mighty hand we live and by whose loving care our lives are preserved, we thank You for Your protection during the night now past and for the privilege of another day of life in Your service. Grant to us and our loved ones Your continued presence. Protect our homes, our schools, our community, and our nation from harm. Graciously preserve us from temptation and sin. We ask Your special blessing upon those who are in any distress of body, mind, or spirit; help them experience Your ready help and loving comfort.

As we return to our daily work, keep our occupations from becoming drudgery, and remove from them all tension and boredom. Give us a new vision of our tasks — as opportunities for worshiping You and as vocations in which we glorify You by our service.

In Your mercy preserve from defeatism those who are unemployed, unemployable, or retired. Enable them to find in their leisure new opportunities for witness to You and for service to their church. Fill us all with the joy of service, for the sake of Jesus, who went about doing good. Amen.

Tuesday Evening

Almighty God, Giver of every good and perfect gift, hear us this evening as we turn our hearts and minds to You in quiet prayer. Today again You cheered us with the sunshine of Your love, the security of Your presence, and the joy of Your blessing upon all we did for You. Forgive us the failures of this day, especially our failure to appreciate good health as Your gift.

We ask Your special blessing upon Your many ministers of mercy among us: the doctors who diagnose and treat our ills; the nurses who contribute to our physical comfort in sickness; the pharmacists and laboratory technicians who compound the medications and administer the tests and treatments. Give them the awareness that their devotion to duty is known to You. Help us all to appreciate health in greater measure, to safeguard it as a precious gift, and to use our strength and talents to serve Your divine purposes.

And now surround us this night with a cordon of Your heavenly hosts, that no evil may come near us and no harm befall us. Hear us for the sake of Jesus, the great Healer. Amen.

Wednesday Morning

Gracious Lord, Your mercies are new to us every morning. Great is Your faithfulness. We thank You for refreshing sleep and for Your watchful care during the night. With Your all-seeing eye upon us, protect us from harm this day. Help us to think, desire, speak, and do only what is right and pleasing to You. Keep us mindful of the many blessings we enjoy as citizens of our free country.

In these difficult times, O Lord, give wisdom and guidance especially to our President, to the members of his cabinet and of Congress, as well as to all who occupy places of public trust and positions of authority in our land. Cause them at all times to seek Your providential will, and give them courage to follow it.

Lead our citizens to turn to You in repentance and faith. If it be Your will, continue to bless us with abundant natural resources and material prosperity. But, above all, give us the grace to share them with the needy in our ghettos and with those in want throughout the world. We ask this in the name of Jesus, who had no place where to lay His head. Amen.

Wednesday Evening

O Lord of light, as darkness falls upon another day, our hearts are moved to turn to You in prayer. Dispel the darkness of sin from our hearts, and by Your Spirit grant us the assurance that we are Your forgiven children through the shed blood of Jesus Christ. Pardon our faults and failures of this day, our irritableness under pressure, our impatience with those with whom we live and work, our inept words blurted out only to be regretted. Erase them from the tablet of Your memory, O Lord, and record them no longer against us.

As we are about to lie down to refreshing sleep, we think of those who must work this night: those who fly our planes, run our trains, and drive our buses and trucks; the policemen, firemen, and night watchmen who guard us. Be with them as they do their duty in darkness. Keep them alert to their tasks. But above all, remind us that You who keep Israel neither slumber nor sleep and that all who trust in You will never be alone.

Keep us all beneath the shadow of Your protecting wing, and claim us always as Your own by faith in Christ, our Savior. Amen.

Thursday Morning

With the rising sun we come to You, Lord God, at the beginning of this uncharted day. Make Your Word a lamp to our feet and a light to our way. By Your Spirit help us to make the right choices in life, to lead others in paths pleasing to You, and always to reveal the mind of Christ. Fill our hearts with compassion for the straying and lost, that by Your grace we may lead them to the cross of our beloved Redeemer. Look with favor upon the preachers and teachers of the Gospel as they proclaim Christ to the nations.

Bless our missionaries and all frontline workers in their efforts to spread the Gospel throughout the world. Give them courage in the face of danger, strength in their weakness, and encouragement when the harvest of Your Word is slow to appear. Keep their families safe from harm, and fill them with joy for the task they share. Grant the heathen grace to accept in faith the message of heavenly peace in Christ. Increase our interest in and support of the work of evangelizing the world. For the sake of Jesus, whose witnesses we are. Amen.

Thursday Evening

Eternal God, Sun of our soul, light and darkness are alike to You. As we prepare for rest and sleep this night, cleanse us from all sin. Help us to enjoy the peace of a good conscience and the quietness of an untroubled mind, which blessings come from a life that is one with Christ.

In the evening hour of this day we offer our prayers on behalf of our youth. May the mind of Jesus as a lad motivate them in all their attitudes and actions. By Your Holy Spirit help them to know and obey You as their heavenly Father. Lead them to appreciate the love and concern of their parents and the blessings of a Christian home. Teach them as responsible young people to prepare for the larger obligations of the future and to discharge the duties of life with courage and faithfulness. Protect them in the hour of temptation, give them a sense of purpose in living, and help them to find their identity in You.

Graciously watch over all Your children everywhere, and keep them in Your love and favor this night. This we ask in Jesus' name. Amen.

Friday Morning

Lord Jesus Christ, on this morning when we remember that You were crucified for us, draw us in sincere repentance to Your cross, there to find forgiveness for our sins, strength for every trial, comfort in sorrow, and peace amidst the uncertainties of life. You died for us; grant that we may daily die to the sins of our flesh. You rose again from the dead; help us rise from sin and make us new creatures of Your redemptive love.

Waken within us the love and concern which You have for all men. We pray for all who are wronged or oppressed, the members of minority groups who suffer from injustice, the poor and deprived in the ghettos of our cities. Keep them from bitterness, anger, violence, and despair.

In Your compassion be with all who are friendless and homeless, with displaced persons and refugees, with derelicts and the forgotten of today's indifferent society, with the emotionally and mentally disturbed.

Comfort those who have lost dear ones, and give us the empathy that suffers with those who suffer. For Your sake, the Suffering Servant of God. Amen.

Friday Evening

Dear heavenly Father, the death and burial of Your Son remind us of the evening hour of our lives. As Jesus on this day completed His work of redemption on the cross, so help us to lay aside tonight our completed tasks. As He unburdened Himself of our sins that Good Friday, so may the Holy Spirit remove from us our failures, discouragements, and frustrations. As our Lord committed Himself into Your hands for the repose of death, so we commit ourselves to Your care for sweet rest and sleep this night.

As we go to bed, remind us of the day when we shall lie upon our beds for the last time, so that, entrusting ourselves always to You, we shall awaken from our last sleep to be forever with You. Meanwhile, as day and night, work and rest alternate throughout our earthly years, make the death and resurrection of Christ, our Lord, the source of our confidence and the guarantee of our peace. Then at the great resurrection give us through Christ the perfect rest, joy, and peace of heaven. Amen.

Saturday Morning

As another week draws to a close, we thank You, gracious Lord, for Your multiplied blessings, which are new to us each morning. Lead us to number them one by one, as well as our days.

The rapid flight of time reminds us especially of Your loving protection of Your children everywhere. Today we commend to Your gracious care and concern the men and women who have been called to serve our country on land and sea and in the air. Strengthen their faith. Protect them in danger. Shield them from temptation. Go with them, wherever their course of duty may take them, as their Companion in loneliness, their Counselor in doubt, their Healer in sickness, their Strength in weakness, and their Friend in every need. Assure them that since they are Your children, redeemed by the blood of Christ, all things will work together for their good.

O God of peace, preside over the counsels of world leaders, overrule the evil designs of selfish men in their struggle for power, and establish lasting peace among the nations of the earth; for Jesus' sake. Amen.

Saturday Evening

Lord God, our Help in ages past, our Hope for years to come, we thank You for all the blessings of life, especially for the new life in Christ and for the hope of immortality in glory. In gratitude for Your unnumbered favors help us in the future to live not to ourselves but to Your glory and for the welfare of all whom our lives may touch.

As another week sinks into eternity, we pray for our family and for all the families in Your great family in the world. Turn the hearts of parents to their children and the hearts of children to their parents in loving concern for each other's welfare. Induce husbands and wives tenderly to serve each other for their mutual benefit, that the homes they build may be a foretaste of our home in heaven, where we shall all be with You, our heavenly Father.

Cradle us in Your everlasting arms this night, and permit us to awaken tomorrow, on the Lord's day, refreshed and strengthened to sing Your praises with our families and the company of believers in our houses of worship, for Jesus' sake. Amen.

Sunday Morning

Lord, heavenly Father,
We thank You for this blessed day,
    because You have made it holy for us.
We thank You for this day as a new beginning,
    because this day You began creation.
We thank You for this day of renewal,
    because this day You raised our Lord.
We thank You for this day of grace,
    because this day You poured out Your
        Spirit.
Bless our worship this day as we
    see anew the gifts of Your creation.
Restore to us the joy of Your salvation
    through our living Lord Jesus Christ.
Grant to us the power of a continuing
    Pentecost through Your Word and sac-
        raments.
Make us not only hearers of Your Word
    but also doers to the praise of Your glory,
    in Christ Jesus, our Lord. Amen.

Sunday Evening

Lord God, heavenly Father,
Bless the Word which passed between
    preachers and hearers this day.
Accept the psalms and hymns
    and spiritual songs offered as praise.
Give ear to the prayers
    spoken at altars in every place.
Sanctify all the gifts
    placed at Your feet.
Strengthen all who feasted
    at Your table.
Seal in the covenant of Your love
    all who were washed in the name of Christ.
Grant peace to Your children everywhere
    who call on Your name this day,
        through Jesus Christ, our Lord. Amen.

Monday Morning

Heavenly Father,
We thank You for the privilege of work.
Use our talents and energies
    in Your service for our fellowman.
Help us to see our tasks
    as expressions of trust from You.
Keep us from seeing our chores
    as cumbersome duties and toil.
Remind us we are doing more
    than merely making a living.
Give us the joy in Christ
    to do all things to Your glory.
Enable us to see in all our tasks that we
    are called as laborers in Your vineyard.
Keep us faithful and useful to all
    as men and women who have only one
        Lord,
    even Jesus Christ, our Savior. Amen.

Monday Evening

Creator God,
We thank and praise You
    because of Your love in Your creation.
Forgive our misuse, abuse, and neglect
    of that which sustains life.
Forgive our failures, mistakes, and errors
    in serving those who need us.
Forgive our dislikes, distaste, and the omission
    of that which is essential.
Accept our efforts at service
    in which we have done our best.
Accept our labors for others
    in which we did all we could.
Accept our products of love
    in which we gave of ourselves.
In Jesus, our Lord, give us rest tonight,
    and refresh us to begin tomorrow anew
    in His name and for His sake. Amen.

Tuesday Morning

Heavenly Father,
We thank You for rest and strength.
Renew us for service
    by the renewal of our minds in
    Christ Jesus.
As He was humble and obedient even to
      death,
    make us humble and obedient to You.
We also pray for all laborers
    in homes, in industry, and in the
    professions.
Keep all workers mindful
    that we are dependent on one another.
Give all who serve genuine love
    with strength and wisdom.
Enable men everywhere to serve in unity,
    that righteousness may prevail.
Cause all men to work at their tasks
    for the blessing of the whole society.
We pray in the name
    of Jesus Christ, our Lord. Amen.

Tuesday Evening

Lord God, heavenly Father,
Use the quiet of this night
    to settle the hearts of men everywhere,
    that they may contemplate
    Your goodness and Your mercy.
Still the strife that enters
    homes, communities, and nations.
Put down those who
    employ power for power's sake.
Stifle the mouths of those who
    foment bigotry and hate.
Pour out Your love in fullness
    upon those who honor Your name,
    that Your kingdom may come
    and Your will may be done
    among us, for Jesus' sake. Amen.

Wednesday Morning

Heavenly Father,
Give us the grace in Christ
   not to become weary in well-doing.
Keep us mindful that we
   shall reap if we faint not.
Keep us from fretfulness of spirit
   that would dull our work.
Help us take the yoke of Christ cheerfully,
   because He makes the burden lighter.
Remember today all who cannot work:
   the sick, the aged, the infirm,
   the shut-ins, the mentally ill,
   the incompetent, and those who
   cannot find employment.
Help us remember that to help them
   is a privilege and trust from You.
Give us compassion to share with
   the least of our Lord's brothers.
Accept what we do for them as
   done unto Him, in whose name we pray.
   Amen.

Wednesday Evening

Holy Father,
We glorify Your name
   because You give rest to the weary.
Strengthen this night
   all who are worn from the burdens
   of labor.
Relieve through Him who died for all
   those who are sick and dying.
Comfort with the news of the Resurrection
   those who mourn.
Counsel with the wisdom of Your love
   those who are in difficulty.
Cheer with the joy of salvation
   those who are depressed.
Renew with the assurance of Your presence
   those who are lonely.
Send the angels of Your mercy
   to those who are distressed.
Reach out to all men this night
   with the healing and redeeming
   love of Christ, our Lord. Amen.

Thursday Morning

Heavenly Father,
We remember today
    we do not live by our own efforts.
We live from Your open hand,
    which sustains every living thing.
We live also by that Word
    which proceeds from Your mouth.
Remember therefore also those
    who labor for us in Your kingdom.
Bless pastors, teachers, and missionaries
    with the power of Your Spirit.
Keep all servants of Your Word
    from all harm and danger.
Give them courage to proclaim
    the Gospel with boldness and power.
Help us to support them constantly
    with our prayers and gifts.
Help us to share with them
    the peace that passes all understanding.
So shall our hearts and minds
    be kept in Christ Jesus. Amen.

Thursday Evening

Gracious God,
We pray You to watch over all who serve You
    in every land and every place.
Guard all who carry Your Gospel
    into remote places at great cost.
Strengthen those who suffer
    and are persecuted for Your name's sake.
Bless those who preach, teach, counsel,
    and administer in the name of Christ.
Multiply the fruits of the labor of all
    who confess Your name before men.
Imbue all Your people baptized in Christ
    with devotion, love, and zeal.
Enable all Your adopted children
    to serve Your will in the variety
    of their vocations, arts, and crafts,
    that men may see their good works
    and glorify You through Christ, our Lord,
    in whose name we pray. Amen.

Friday Morning

Heavenly Father,
We thank You this day
    for the good You have prepared for us
    by the suffering and death of Your Son.
Cause Him, who is our Life and our Salvation,
    to be our Example and our Guide,
    that we may seek not to be served
    but to serve.
Remember Your children everywhere
    as You keep them in their baptismal grace.
Help us put to death the old nature,
    as we were buried with Christ in baptism.
Raise us again to new life,
    as we are risen with Christ in baptism.
Help us to grow in knowledge,
    that Christ may be formed in us.
In His name we pray. Amen.

Friday Evening

Almighty God,
We confess that we have sinned against You
    through our doubts and despair,
    through our anxieties and neglect,
    through our rebellion and selfishness.
Have mercy on us
    through Your Son, who died for us.
Forgive us
    through Him who rose again for us.
Give us peace
    through Him who is our Peace.
Strengthen us against temptation
    through Him who overcame the Tempter.
Sustain us in trouble
    through Him who is our Help.
Guard us this night
    that in the morning
    we may wake in the joy of Your love,
    which You give us through Christ. Amen.

Saturday Morning

Gracious Father,
Because You have created us
    anew by Your Holy Spirit,
Accept us, the work of our hands,
    and all that we have.
Grant that at all times
    we entrust to You our lives.
Receive what we are and do
    as living sacrifices in Christ.
Make us and keep us
    wholly Yours in Him.
What we give to You we offer
    in faith in You and love for the neighbor.
Hear us and accept our all
    for the sake of Your Son, our Lord. Amen.

Saturday Evening

O Lord, our God,
Because You have called us in love,
  forgive our failure to be loving.
Because You have called us in freedom,
  forgive our hesitancy to serve.
Use this night to refresh us
  with zest and desire to do good.
May this night not be darkened
  by the failures of the past week.
Let the hope You have given us in Christ
  shine brightly into the dawning of a new
    day.
Tomorrow help us to be born anew
  through the grace of Your Word,
  in Christ Jesus, our Lord. Amen.

Luther's Morning Prayer

In the name of the Father and of the Son
and of the Holy Ghost. Amen.

I thank You, my heavenly Father,
through Jesus Christ, Your dear Son,
that You have kept me this night from all
harm and danger;
and I pray You that You would keep me this
day also from sin and every evil,
that all my doings and life may please You.
For into Your hands I commend myself,
my body and soul, and all things.
Let Your holy angel be with me,
that the wicked Foe may have no power over
me. Amen.

Luther's Evening Prayer

In the name of the Father and of the Son
and of the Holy Ghost. Amen.

I thank You, my heavenly Father,
     through Jesus Christ, Your dear Son,
that You have graciously kept me this day;
and I pray You that You would forgive me
all my sins where I have done wrong,
and graciously keep me this night.
For into Your hands I commend myself,
my body and soul, and all things.
Let Your holy angel be with me,
that the wicked Foe may have no power over
     me. Amen.

PRAYERS
FOR
MY LIFE OF WORSHIP

Remembrance of Baptism

Lord God, I am Your child. I call You Father because You are my Father. You named me with Your own holy name even before I could speak. You made me Your own before I could move a hand to help or prevent You. You insisted on having me even though You knew the end of my life as well as its beginning, its shame as well as its glory, its failures as well as its achievements, its bad as well as its good.

Why, Father, should I persist in resisting You? Why should I insist on my own way instead of knowing Your way of grace and love? Why should I obey my own whims instead of letting Your grace in baptism have its way with me?

Forgive me, Father, for so often wandering into a far country away from You, Your forgiveness, Your joy, Your promises, Your love in Jesus Christ. Help me to live in the freedom of my baptism, by the faith of my sonship, in the life which You daily renew by Your gracious forgiveness.

I am baptized. I belong to You, God. Abba, Father! Abba, dear Father! Amen.

Confession

It is hard for me, O God, to confess my sins and not merely repeat well-worn phrases with which I try to cover my real guilt.

I am a sinner. Why is it so difficult for me to see that, Lord? Why am I so bothered with a few things I do wrong while I think nothing of my lack of trust in You? Why do I feel guilty when I do not live up to my own standards but hardly blush when I fail You? Why do I imitate unholy men instead of following the Christ? I must confess it is because I follow my own desires, because I am weak in the face of temptations, and without You I am nothing.

All I can do is plead mercy, O God. I cannot even hold up the honesty and fullness of my confession. All I can do is trust Your love in Jesus Christ. I surely cannot trust my love for You or for Him. Hear me for the sake of Jesus Christ, who lived for me and died that in Him I might live.

Forgive me, Father! Forgive me even this, my poor confession. I need Your forgiveness for Christ's sake. Amen.

Before Communion

O Bread of Life from heaven:
I confess that I have tasted
    the bread that does not satisfy,
    the meat that perishes,
    the sweet fruits of temptation,
    the bitters of my guilt.
I thank and praise You
    that You offer the bread
        which is not bread alone,
    that You offer the wine
        from the winepress You trod alone,
    that You offer the Holy Meal
        which is Your body and Your blood.
I pray:
    forgive my unworthiness;
    create in me faith in Your love;
    enable me to taste of Your mercy.
So shall I be restored to the health
    of Your salvation. Amen.

After Communion

Lord God of mercy, at the table
    You prepared in the face of my enemies
I give You thanks
    for the body and blood of Your Son,
        the pledge of my salvation;
    for the Word by which
        You give me forgiveness;
    for Your promises by which
        You give me life.
May the gifts of Your heavenly banquet
    fortify me against the Evil One,
    strengthen me in the face of the world,
    overcome my selfishness.
Help me to live as one
    who hungers for Your grace,
    who thirsts after righteousness,
    who longs to taste of Your goodness,
    that I may sit at Your table
    at the marriage feast when
    the heavenly Bridegroom comes
    to take His holy bride to Himself. Amen.

Before Worship

Lord God, revealed to Moses in a burning bush, to Israel in a cloudy pillar, to Isaiah on a lofty throne: help us in our worship to stand before You as on holy ground, seek the company of Your grace, hear and obey the voice of Your Word. Remove from us all hindrances to proper confession and forgiveness, to attentive hearing and obedience, to sincere praise and thanksgiving, that we may go forth with Your benediction; through Christ, our Lord. Amen.

After Worship

Heavenly Father, Creator of all things by Your Word, we thank You that You have planted the seed of Your Word in our hearts and nourished it with Your grace, and that You are able to make the seed bring forth and bud. Root out all matter alien to Your will, cultivate our hearts with Your mercy, and water the seed with the showers of Your love, so will we bring forth the fruits of repentance, of faith, and of hope. Hear us for the sake of Your Son Jesus Christ, who died that He might bring forth life in us. Amen.

PRAYERS
FOR
USE IN THE CHURCH YEAR

Advent

Lord God, we praise You that You comforted Your people with the promise of a Redeemer. We praise You that in the fullness of time You sent Your Son as the Redeemer. We praise You that You give promise that You will send Him to us again to judge the world in righteousness.

Open our hearts to receive our Redeemer now as He comes to us in Word and Sacrament. Open our eyes in awareness of His rule in our lives by His grace.

Make Advent a blessing to us as we welcome our King in faith and love. We lift up our heads to welcome Him anew. Fill us with gladness as He comes to us. Amen.

Advent

God of the covenant, we give You glory and honor for sending Your Son Jesus Christ to fulfill all Your promises. By Your grace send us now preachers of repentance who will make us a people prepared to receive Him in faith. Lead us to rejoice in His coming in the flesh to accomplish all things for our salvation. Fill us with hope that we may be in constant readiness for the day of His coming again. Grant us Your Spirit that we may live as those who know that He who has come is with us now, that we may be with Him when all shall behold His coming. In His name we ask it. Amen.

Christmas Eve

Heavenly Father, we thank You for the holy gift You gave us when You stooped down to our world to place in the arms of a mother the gift of Your Son. We confess that by our sin we insult His innocence. By our doubts we mock His trust of Your Word. By our selfishness we make light of His sacrifice. Forgive us, and renew in us trust in Your love and grace through Your most holy Son.

Hallow this night, Lord, that it may be Your holy night for us. Help us hear Your angel speak through Your Word, that we may no longer live in fear. Lead us to listen to the Gospel, Your Good News, that we may know Your Son born to us: the Savior, Christ the Lord. Open our hearts to hear the mighty choirs sing of all Your promises, that we may see Your glory in the highest in Christ's humble birth, and Your peace for us and for all men in His lowly coming. Let Him who once was born be born anew in us this night. Amen.

Christmas Day

Lord Jesus, because You became a babe, we can pray to You and know that God in heaven hears us. As a babe you are Immanuel, God-with-us, God-in-our-place. For this we most heartily thank You, for now we know the God of all love, the God who has drawn close to us that we might draw close to Him.

How wonderfully You came to take away all our fear and all our doubts! You came as a babe helpless to be our Help. You came as a babe humble to remove our pride. You came as a babe lowly so that we might be lifted up to You. You came as a babe pure so that You might take upon Yourself our sin.

Help us, Lord, to know You always as You are, so that we need no longer seek far and wide, high and low to find God. Fill us with Your Spirit and bring us again to kneel at Your manger, there to confess: "My Lord and my God!" Amen.

New Year's Eve

Lord, we hailed bravely the beginning of the year now almost past. We took this year, all bright and shiny, from Your hand and determined that it would be different from all others. We were eager to fill it with good things, so that we proudly could hand it back to You this night.

Now, Lord, see what we have done! The year shows that for the most part we do not improve with the passage of time but only become older sinners instead.

As the clock once again strikes twelve tonight, can we join in the gaiety? The sound of the gong could well be our death knell in the new year. Nevertheless, Lord, we come before You in the hope that Jesus offers, because He came into the world to save sinners.

In this spirit we offer our broken and our contrite hearts. These You will not despise. Lord, we have no time, past, present, or future, except Christ's time for us: forgiven time behind us and with us, hope-filled time before us. Only in Christ's time can we live, because His time is grace. Amen.

New Year's Day

Lord God, heavenly Father, though You have created us for a life of eternity, we confess that by our sins we have transformed the space of time into a prelude for death. Forgive us the sins of the past, and breathe into us the Spirit of Your Son that we may serve You in this new year.

On this first day of a new year pour into our hearts the rich measure of Your grace, that we may fill the moments of the new year with the enduring qualities of eternity. On this day You placed Your Son under the Law to fulfill all righteousness for us; make us Your obedient children. On this day our Lord was given His name according to Your Word; may we also be known by His name.

In Him we find courage to begin again. He is our Beginning and our End, our Alpha and our Omega. In Him is our hope. In Him this year and all things are made new because we are forgiven. For His sake help us to live for You and our fellowman. Amen.

Epiphany

Lord Jesus Christ, the Light of the world, help us so to follow You that we may never walk in darkness but have the light of life.

As men were led by the brightness of Your light to come and worship You, illumine our hearts that the veil of darkness and death may be lifted from our eyes and we may see the salvation of our God.

We believe that You are the Word made flesh and that You dwell among us. Use this blessed season to help us see Your glory, the glory as of the Only-begotten of the Father, that You may be grace and truth to us.

Increase in us the desire to support with our gifts and prayers the missions to men everywhere who have not seen the light, that Your kingdom may ring with praises for You from men of every tribe, nation, kindred, and tongue. We ask it in Your name. Amen.

Ash Wednesday

Lord Jesus, we come before You sprinkled with ashes of sorrow, robed in sackcloth of repentance, and humbled by our fault, by our most grievous fault.

We slept when You urged us to watch. We sought comfort when You urged us to pray. We followed afar off when You wanted us near You. We betrayed You when You were bearing witness to the truth in our behalf. We fled when You assured us that our only safety is in You.

Lord, we are deeply involved in Your Passion. We need only look at Your disciples to see ourselves. But the important thing is that we see You. Through bloody sweat You prayed to do the will of the Father. You drained the cup which we filled for You, and now there is not a drop left for us to drink. For this we humbly and heartily thank You, Lord, and pray that we may live continually in this gratitude.

Help us so to watch with You in Your Passion, that we remain awake to the infinite power of Your love. Amen.

Lent

Lord, bring us close to Your cross that we might know how You loved us and gave Yourself for us.

We would keep Lent, Lord, in a way that is pleasing to You. As we follow You from the garden to Calvary, do not let us follow afar off, lest we deny You. Help us watch and pray with You that we may not fall into temptation.

Enlighten us that we may see by faith that You knelt in prayer for us, that You, the Holy One, were judged a criminal by unholy men for us, that You suffered the whiplashes of angry sinners as our sinless Savior, that You stumbled under the cross as our Suffering Servant, that you died as the Lamb of God in our stead and for our sake.

Lord Jesus, through it all help us hear in Your prayer the single purpose for which You endured pain and death: "Father, forgive them, for they know not what they do." Amen.

Palm Sunday

Lord, the Day of Palms is a day of triumph in Your life. As You set Your face toward death and moved to the hour of Your glory beyond the cross, You came to us as King. Yet You came in lowly pomp that we might know the real purpose of Your coming.

Amid the shouts of "Hosannah to the Son of David" we know You as the Suffering Servant of God.

Through the waving palm branches we see You as the King of our peace.

On the way paved with the garments of man's homage we see You as the Son of Man, who came not to be served but to serve and to give His life a ransom for many.

Among the chants and songs of praises of little children we know You as the One who came to make us the children of God.

Come, King of grace, to rule in us. Lord of all mercy, have mercy upon us. Savior of sinners, save us. Amen.

Maundy Thursday

We remember, Lord, that on this night in which You were betrayed You provided the blessed meal of Your Holy Supper for us. On the eve of the most dreadful hours of Your life, we should think of what You were facing. But You did not think of Yourself. You thought of us, You cared for us, and You remembered us so that we could remember often what You have done for our salvation.

At Your table, Lord, we join the whole company of believers who feast on Your mercy. Unite us in the fellowship of faith as we are made one in this common meal. Make us participants in the victory which You won by the sacrifice of Your body and blood. Seal to us the eternal fruits of salvation that You promised with the giving of this meal.

May this holy supper always be to us the Holy Eucharist, the holy giving of thanks, that we may find the joy which You provided for us by Your sorrow. Accept now our thanks, Lord, and keep alive in us the hope that we shall break bread with You in eternity. Amen.

Good Friday

O Christ, the Lamb of God that takes away the sin of the world, have mercy upon us.

O Christ, the Lamb of God that takes away the sin of the world, have mercy upon us.

O Christ, the Lamb of God, that takes away the sin of the world. grant us Your peace.

We thank and praise You that on this day

> You prayed the Father for our forgiveness;
>
> You promised us Paradise;
>
> You placed us in loving relationship with each other;
>
> You were forsaken of God, that we may never be forsaken;
>
> You finished all things necessary for our salvation;
>
> You committed Your spirit to the Father that we may die in peace.

Give us faith to glory in Your cross, by which we may overcome every evil and finally gain full and complete victory in Your name. Amen.

Holy Saturday

Heavenly Father, we are silenced at the grave of Your Son. In justice You called for Him, who knew no sin, to be made sin for us. Yet You permitted Your Son to die in innocence. In love He came to us but He was rejected by hate. He taught us obedience but men rebelled against Him.

We confess that a great mystery confronts us at this tomb of sin and death. He was buried behind the great seal of our sin and our death. By faith we know also that He who died is the One who unlocked the great secret of Your love. His tomb is our tomb. He carried with Him to the grave our sin and our death that He might break their hold on us.

Trusting in our Lord's promise that He would rise again on the third day, we come not to mourn Him but to confess the sin that He would leave buried. Have mercy on us! Grant us the Easter faith that anticipates with joy the day on which You raised Him from the dead, so that in Him we too shall come forth from the tomb to live with Him in eternity. We pray in His name and for His sake. Amen.

Easter

The Lord is risen! He is risen indeed! Hallelujah! Heavenly Father, we worship You and adore You because You have raised Your Son from the dead and made Him to be Lord over all things in heaven and in earth.

Fill us with confidence that in the risen Christ we can overcome all threats to the reality of Your love for us. Especially destroy in us the fear that death separates us from Your mercy.

We long for some proof, like touching the risen One. Comfort us with His assurance and benediction that we are blessed as a people not seeing and yet believing. We yearn to roll away the stone of all our doubts. Help us see in the empty tomb that the stone is already rolled away, that we no longer seek the living One among the dead.

Give us of Your Spirit that we may live under Your Son in the freedom of those who have been delivered from death to life. Raise us each day from the depths of sin to the joys of forgiveness, and let us walk before You in righteousness; through our risen Lord and Redeemer. Amen.

Ascension

Lord God, heavenly Father, we thank and praise You that You raised Your Son from the dead, seated Him at Your right hand, and placed all things under His feet that He might rule in majesty. You have crowned Him with glory as our King of kings and Lord of lords.

Fulfill for us His promise that He would be with us always, even to the end of the world. Fill us with His Spirit to carry out His commission to make disciples of all nations as You have made us His disciples. Even as You have drawn Him to Yourself, so draw us to Him. As He returned to You to prepare a place for us, so take us to Yourself at His coming again. We come to You boldly in prayer, as He invited us to do when He ascended on high. Amen.

Pentecost

Lord God, we praise You for the gift of Your Spirit, whom You poured upon fearful men to make them bold witnesses of the mighty acts You accomplished through Your holy Son Jesus, the Christ.

Give us the power of Your Spirit that we may serve You without fear. Regenerate us by Your Spirit that we may live each day as new persons in Christ. Fill us with Your Spirit that we may reach out in love to all men. Work in us with Your Spirit that we may always do Your will. Help us to see our baptism as the seal of the Spirit and the pledge of greater gifts to come.

By Your gracious gift of faith enable us to walk in the Spirit and to live in hope. Seal us in Spirit that we may be Yours eternally.

We pray through Him who promised that You would send the Spirit in His name. Amen.

Trinity

Holy God, triune God, the true and living God, the one and only Lord of all, accept our worship and adoration. Though we cannot understand, we join the seraphim in covering our eyes and our feet in deepest reverence, and in crying: "Holy, holy, holy, Lord God of hosts! Heaven and earth are full of Your glory!" Yet in Jesus Christ we know You, because in Him You have made Yourself known.

God the Father, we adore You because You made Yourself our Father in Jesus Christ and sealed Your fatherhood to us in baptism.

God the Son, we praise You because You became flesh, that we might see the glory of God in Your life and death for us.

God the Holy Spirit, we trust You because You led us to know Jesus Christ and covered us with His holiness.

We confess You, O triune God, in the power of Your majesty. To You alone be all glory now and forever. Amen.

Reformation

Heavenly Father, we heartily thank You for Your gift of Martin Luther to Your church. Your church would soon perish on the face of the earth if You did not continually reform it. Make us true children of the Reformation today through repentance and faith, through loyalty and diligence. Help us be Your people by being what we are through Your grace in Christ Jesus. Cause us to stand only in the faith of Jesus Christ as our Savior and our Lord, the true Rock of the church.

Bring us to know You as You have made Yourself known by the Spirit through the Holy Scriptures, that we may become wise unto salvation through faith which is in Christ Jesus.

Give us grace to come always to You on behalf of the church and our fellowmen, because You are able to do exceeding abundantly above all that we ask or think according to the power that works in us. So shall we give You alone all glory in the church by Christ Jesus, both now and forever. Amen.

Day of Humiliation and Prayer

Heavenly Father, we come before You weighed down by our sins, our known and unknown guilt, our part in causing the miseries of our bleeding times. We have not always been loyal to our Lord Jesus Christ. We have not spoken the Word of His forgiveness and peace to others as we ought. We have not lived as children of Your holy family as we should.

To whom shall we turn if we cannot run to You? We humble ourselves under Your mighty hand which rests heavily upon us. We are ashamed and defenseless.

But there is forgiveness with You, Father, for we pray in the name of Jesus Christ, our Savior. In Him we know that You love us and have redeemed us. In Him we learn that You bring us down only to raise us up, and make us nothing only to create us anew. We wait on You, Father. Restore to us the joy of Your salvation, and uphold us with Your strengthening Spirit. Though You slay us, yet will we trust in You, for we have no other hope or help than You. Hear us for the sake of Your Son, Jesus Christ, our Lord. Amen.

PRAYERS
FOR
THE CHURCH

For the Church

O God, because You elected from eternity to
    save us from destroying ourselves;
We praise You
    that You gave promise of salvation
        to Adam and his seed;
    that You saved Noah and his family
        in the ark of faith;
    that You protected and saved
        ancient Israel as Your people.
We give You thanks
    that You saved mankind
        by the death and resurrection
        of our Lord, the Christ;
    that You extended Your kingdom
        to many tribes and nations;
    that You have preserved Your Word
        in the Holy Scriptures.
We pray You,
    rule in our hearts by faith;
    promote unity among us by love;
    seal in us the hope of the Resurrection.
Finish Your work among us through Your
    Word and sacraments, for Jesus' sake.
    Amen.

For Unity in the Church

Heavenly Father,
You called us into the body of Christ:
> Help us live as one in Him.

You have given us one faith:
> Keep us in the one true faith.

You have given us one baptism:
> Let us live in our common baptismal grace.

You have given us apostles and prophets:
> Let us hear with singleness of heart.

You have sent us pastors and teachers:
> Enlighten us to learn with oneness of mind.

You have equipped us for the unity of faith:
> Help us attain that unity by forgiveness.

You have given us Your love in Christ:
> Enable us to speak Your truth in love.

You built Your church of Your will:
> Make us to fit into our proper place.

You create Your church of living stones:
> Enliven us to serve Your holy purpose,
> that the whole church may grow and
> upbuild itself in love.

We ask it in the name of Jesus, the chief
Shepherd and Bishop of our souls. Amen.

For Missions

O God of infinite grace and love,
  because Your Son died for all men,
  because You grieve over the death of
    the wicked,
  because You would draw all men to You:
We confess that we have not
  spoken of Your love as we ought,
  supported Your work as we are able,
  sacrificed for Your cause as we might.
We urge You to
  remove the indifference of our hearts,
  stir in us the cheerfulness of generosity,
  strengthen us to surrender ourselves to
    You.
We pray for those who
  speak for You in foreign lands,
  spread Your name through every medium,
  suffer for Your Gospel's sake.
We beseech You to
  let Your Word be fruitful in every land,
  dispel the gloom of ignorance and sin,
  loosen tongues to sing Your praise.
Bless all who labor, that Your name be
    hallowed
  in all the earth, for Jesus' sake. Amen.

For Ministers

Lord God, revealed in the preaching of Jesus
    at the seashore,
    in the city and highway,
    in home and upper room,
    in synagog and temple,
    in mountain and wilderness,
    to sick and despondent,
    to sinner and outcast,
    to soldier and ruler,
    to alien and pilgrim,
    to rich and poor;
Because You have commanded us
    to preach Your Gospel to the nations,
    to shout it from the housetops,
    to speak it in the light,
    to bring Your peace to all,
    to announce the coming of Your kingdom:
We pray You,
    use our ministers of the Word
    to speak judgment and
    to proclaim forgiveness of sins
    for the salvation of many. Amen.

For Teachers

Lord God, because You have given us
  the gift of reason to solve problems,
  the gift of memory to recall our past,
  the gift of imagination to be creative:
Forgive us
  for our indifference to thinking,
  for our refusal to learn from yesteryears,
  for our failure to use our talents.
Help us to cherish
  the inheritance of great thought,
  the legacy of history,
  the treasure of the arts.
Bless
  our teachers who stimulate thinking,
  our teachers who interpret the record,
  our teachers who inspire artistry.
Strengthen our teachers
  with joyful zeal for their tasks,
  with proper rewards for their efforts.
Prompt us to see in all their teaching
  the Christ as the center of our thought,
  the history of our salvation,
  the beauty of Your creation.
We ask it in the name of Your Son. Amen.

For the Congregation

Remember, O Lord, our congregation,
Your people,

    who are nothing without You,
    who need the Word of Your forgiveness,
    who need comfort and solace,
    who need healing and help,
    who need courage and strength,
    who need counsel and guidance,
    who need food and shelter,
    who need correction and admonition,
    who need acceptance and assurance,
    who need zeal and a willing mind,
    who need example and direction,
    who need charity and goodness,
    who need humility and honesty,
    who need liberty and peace,
    who need wisdom and insight,
    who need faith and hope,
    who need love and joy,

For we are Your people gathered by Your
Spirit around Word and sacraments, that
we may be scattered to share Your love
through Christ, our Lord. Amen.

For the Sunday School

Remember, O Lord,
    Your lambs and Your sheep
    And those who feed them.
Help both teachers and pupils to grow
    in their knowledge of the heavenly Father,
    in their likeness to Christ,
    in repentance for sin,
    in trust in Your mercy,
    in the fruits of the Spirit.
Forgive the times
    they fail to learn,
    they are lazy.
Grant to them
    a larger vision of their vocations,
    a deeper understanding of Your creation,
    progress in practical skills.
Make each Sunday school session an opportunity
    to grow in self-understanding,
    to grow in self-control,
    to grow in self-giving.
By Your grace make them lead
    a life worthy of Your name, fully
    pleasing to You through Christ,
    our Lord. Amen.

For Christian Schools

Holy God, revealed of old in many and various
    ways by the prophets and through
    our Lord, the Christ:
Use our Christian schools
    as homes for the indwelling of Your Spirit,
    as centers for the operation of Your grace,
    as laboratories for Your love.
Fill teachers and students
    with eagerness to learn of You,
    with trust in Your faithfulness,
    with the devotion of Your Spirit,
    with patience of scholarship,
    with the readiness of obedience.
Help them to discover daily
    the correction for rebellion,
    the enlightenment for blindness,
    the freedom of forgiveness.
Help them to translate their study
    into active faith,
    into joyful hope,
    into constant love,
    for the sake of Jesus.
We pray in His name. Amen.

For Colleges and Seminaries

Lord God, Giver, Defender, and Redeemer:
We confess that our heritage of learning
 has not removed our fear of ourselves,
 has not served man's best welfare,
 has not always glorified Your creative
   work.
We pray for our colleges and seminaries:
Forgive students by Your grace when
 in the midst of enlightenment they do
   not see Christ, the Light,
 in the world of ideas they lose ideals,
 in the school of learning they close
   minds,
 in the pursuit of wisdom they are
   imprudent.
Fill them with the freedom of Your Spirit
 in the search for knowledge,
 in the quest for justice,
 in the stewardship of talents.
Prepare them for study with the gifts of
 honor mixed with the meekness of Christ,
 courage matched with trust in Your love,
 energy sparked by zeal of the Spirit.
We ask that You give them
 the courage to face all new learning
 with trust in Christ, our Teacher. Amen.

For Catechumens

Lord God,
Renew the strength of the young
    so that they shall rise up
    with wings like eagles.
We pray,
    remember not the sins of their youth,
    forgive any squandering of their early
        years,
    pardon juvenile neglect of duty.
Grant them
    the faith of young Isaac,
    the vision of young Joseph,
    the obedience of young Samuel,
    the vitality of young David,
    the tenderness of young Jonathan,
    the wisdom of young Solomon,
    the courage of young Daniel,
    the zeal of young Timothy.
Deliver them
    from the temptations of youth,
    from unbelief,
    from forgetting their baptism,
    from losing the gift of Your Spirit.
Hear us for the sake of Your own Son,
    who redeemed us by His grace. Amen.

For Those Who Suffer
for the Sake of Truth

Lord God, revealed in the Christ as the One
    whose foolishness is wiser than men and
    whose weakness is stronger than men:
Help those who suffer for the sake of truth
    to find Your strength in their weakness,
    to see Your glory in what is despised,
    to feel Your presence in what is desolate.
Help them to understand
    that in Your gentleness there is power,
    that in Your grace there is strength,
    that in Your forgiveness there is life.
Relieve them
    from torture and pain,
    from strain of the emotions,
    from temptation, danger and agony of soul.
Use their suffering
    for the conversion of those who torment
      them,
    for the strengthening of those who love
      them,
    for the welfare of Your people
      everywhere.
Keep them in Your steadfast love in Christ.
    our Lord, for His sake. Amen.

PRAYERS
FOR
THE NATION

For the Rule of God in the World

Creator of all things in heaven and on earth, visible and invisible, whether thrones or dominions or principalities or authorities,

Ruler through powers, governments, and authorities ordained and instituted to check evil conduct and to encourage good,

King over those who are kings, Lord over those who are lords, Governor of those who are governors, Chief of those who are chiefs of state,

Cause men everywhere to respect law and justice and to create and enforce legislation, that men may rule with fairness. Give wisdom and restraint to those who bear arms in the community or are entrusted with authority for the sake of peace and order. Where men are unjust, inhuman, and cruel, send correction. Where men are at war, send peace. Where men profit at the expense of human welfare, send relief. Give to all peoples a sense of the necessity to live in the freedom of Your Gospel. Silence the ignorance of foolish men, that all may hear Your voice: through Christ, our Lord. Amen.

For the Nation

Ruler of all men, we thank and praise You for permitting a federation of peoples to grow into a nation within our borders. We thank and praise You that You enabled this nation to survive armed conflicts, cold wars, threats and rumors of war, and the uncertainties of life in this nuclear age.

We pray You to make this nation a haven for refugees, for the persecuted and the displaced. We pray You to urge men in our nation to pursue always the search for human freedoms. We pray You to stimulate the leaders of this nation to regulate our government that it will offer hope of freedom for all who swear allegiance to it. We pray You to forgive our sins of pride, bigotry, lawlessness, indifference, and license.

Forgive us for our waste of natural and human resources, for the neglect of our own rights and the rights of others. Enable us to conduct ourselves honorably as citizens and to manage the affairs of government sensibly. Permit this nation to prosper and to fulfill Your purpose to the good of mankind. We pray in the name of Your Son, our Lord. Amen.

For National Integrity

Lord God, Ruler of all men:
We confess
    the unruliness of our nature,
    the disorderly inclinations of our minds,
    the rebellious whims of our hearts.
We recognize
    our need to be guided,
    our need to be ruled,
    our need to be disciplined.
We ask You
    to guide us by just laws,
    to rule us with love,
    to govern us through responsible men,
    to give us judges who are wise,
    to raise up legislators with integrity,
    to appoint executives who are honest.
We pray You,
    help us to exercise our freedoms,
    help us to discharge our obligations,
    help us to hold the law in high regard;
        through the love of our Lord Jesus,
        who was made under the Law
        to become obedient for our sakes.
In His name. Amen.

For Enemies

Savior of all men, who prayed for Your enemies, who died for us while we were yet sinners, who reconciled us to our Father, who taught us to forgive seventy times seven times: we confess that we chafe with bitterness against our enemies and find it difficult to forgive.

We ask you to forgive our hatred and remove our stubbornness. Forgive us also if we have created ill will, if we have given cause for retaliation, if we have disturbed or disrupted relations with other nations or people. Forgive our display of poor citizenship or our show of bad faith.

Give us the sense of what is right and the readiness to negotiate from a position that is just and honest. Give to our enemies a desire for peace, and a yearning to do what is good in Your sight. If there be those who prefer to promote unruliness and trouble among men, put them down from their places of defiance and evil, that the world may have rest and the nations may serve Your purpose and Your will. Amen.

For All Leaders of Nations

O God, You made man in Your own likeness, and You love what You have made. Give to those whom You have placed in the seats of honor and power a sense of awe and humility before You as their Creator and Lord. Help them to see the unity of the human family and to promote it. Enable them to feel the suffering of humankind and to alleviate it. Encourage them to pursue the truth of human history and to learn from it. Give to them the blessing of sound judgment, the skill of making wise decisions, the patience to act in due time, and the tact for being mutually helpful.

Make the conference table a weapon for keeping peace. Use the councils of leaders as the means to counsel for the good of all men. Help the counselors resolve their differences always in the interest of justice among the people they serve. Keep them from national or racial pride that would jeopardize the safety of any nation. Make them Your servants to serve Your will, that they may also serve those for whom Your Son has died. Amen.

For the Head of Government

Gracious and sovereign Lord, we pray for Your servant, the head of our government, that You might keep him faithful to the solemn office with which You have charged him. Strengthen him and uphold him. Guide and direct him to fulfill Your purposes. Give him counsel and aid that he may preserve the integrity and honor of our nation. Give him firmness to maintain law and justice, and determination to strive for peace with all nations. Give him wisdom in the hours of decision. Give him serenity in the face of crises. Give him courage in the moments of danger. Protect him from assassins and ill health. Guard and defend him that he may serve the security and well-being of his people. Make him a leader of a people who will do Your righteous and holy will among the nations of the earth. We ask it in the name of Your most holy Son, our Lord. Amen.

For Diplomats

O eternal Lord God, You alone control the destiny of the world. Use those who have been chosen to negotiate the affairs among nations, that they may serve Your righteous cause among men. Help them to judge rightly between the trivial and the important. Enable them to speak honorably and responsibly. Keep them from oversight and neglect of duty. Prompt them to use their energies to full capacity and their abilities with wisdom. Teach them that diplomacy is more than shrewdness. Furnish them with the insights, the rectitude, the resources, and the gifts that will enable them to represent the nation with nobility and clarity of purpose. Crown their efforts with growth of understanding and goodwill among nations, that Your Gospel may be preached and men come to know the peace which You alone can give through Christ, our Lord. Amen.

For Administrative Officials

Heavenly Father, guardian and keeper of Your people, watch over those who are entrusted with the administration of government. Make them pure and honest. Keep them from temptation and bribery, from favoritism and prejudice, from indolence and neglect of duty. Create in them the earnest desire to serve faithfully. Attend their efforts, that their work may not suffer from mediocrity. Permit them to experience the joys of noble service completed for a grateful people. Encourage cooperation from those who are served and from those who help to serve. Use every willing service and every effort put forth for good government. Bless the rule over Your people, that Your will may be accomplished among them. Promote all things for the good of the kingdom of Your Son, in whose name we pray. Amen.

For Lawmakers

Author of law and justice, raise up men who will fashion and shape laws that will not only check brutality but will also encourage men to live in peace. Keep our lawmakers from enacting laws that are marred by prejudice, favoritism, or inequity. Restrain them from acting hastily or reacting in vengeance. Give them the ability to work for what is necessary to keep the peace, and let them exercise care, lest their laws become impossible burdens.

Enable our lawmakers to foster legislation that provides government with strength and power tempered by justice. Inspire them with the wisdom to write and enact laws that will guarantee safety, protection, and integrity. Cause lawmakers to encourage goodwill among the people, that all citizens may grow in their appreciation of justice. Use the efforts of those who write the laws and those who interpret them for the accomplishment of what is pleasing to You. We ask it in Jesus' name. Amen.

For Officers of the Law

Heavenly Father, we commend to Your care those who enforce law among us. Watch over them. Protect them from harm and danger. Keep them from the temptations to apply force improperly, to use their authority unwisely, to rely on the instruments of coercion exclusively, to yield to bribery or dishonesty. Keep them from rancor or hatred towards those whom they must apprehend. Equip them with the ability to detect the sources of crime and violence. Give them courage when they are in danger. Give them strength as our defenders. Give them gentleness when they serve those who are hurt or neglected. Give them faithfulness to their task. Give them sympathy for those whom they serve. Reward them with the joys of rendering service that conforms to Your most holy will. We pray in Jesus' name. Amen.

For the Community

Watcher and Keeper of Israel:
Attend Your servants
  who enforce the rule,
  who serve the sick,
  who keep the store,
  who teach the young,
  who labor at their craft,
  who minister with Your Word.
Preserve our community
  from recession and depression,
  from epidemic and contagion,
  from misrule and disharmony,
  from fallout and pollution,
  from drought and flood,
  from fire and holocaust.
Help all citizens to work for the common
      good
  through useful inventions,
  through salutary regulation,
  through helpful occupations,
  through wholesome recreation,
  through good manufacturing,
  through meaningful education.
Give them the grace to obey and trust
  Your Word; through Jesus Christ,
  our Lord. Amen.

For Military Leaders

Almighty God, our gracious Father, give protection, guidance, and support to those who lead the military of our nation. Give them powers of logic, judgment, and knowledge for right decisions to conduct the strategies of wars in defense of our country. Inspire them with respect for the men they command and the people they serve. Grant them loyalty to their nation and to the ideals they are called to defend. Keep them from becoming militaristic or using the power of the military for self-glorifying purposes. Restrain them from acting hastily when haste invites international disaster. Prompt them to act quickly when quickness is essential to national safety.

Watch over all who serve under our military leaders on land, in the air, in space, and on the seas. Help us use military installations and the entire enterprise of national defense as the means for the pursuit and maintenance of peace. Prompt all military leaders to cherish the hope for peace among men, and may they do their utmost to insure it. We ask it for the sake of Him who is our Savior and Lord. Amen.

For Responsible Citizenship

Heavenly Father, we thank You for having given us freedom through Your Son to live as citizens of Your kingdom. We pray that by the gift of Your Spirit we may also live honorably and prudently with all men as citizens of the state. Keep us from becoming indiscreet, from acting rashly, from neglecting the rights of others, from willful disobedience and the neglect of just laws, and from all manner of mischief that is harmful to the community.

Give us the readiness to share the burdens of our community, the willingness to attempt solutions to social problems, and the zeal to join in efforts for the common good. Make us effective voices in government through discussion, petition, debate, use of the ballot, and other proper means. Help us accept cheerfully the opportunities for service in the community at every level. Aid us in managing our affairs sensibly. By Your grace enable us to overcome all temptation and do what is pleasing to You by faith in our Lord Jesus Christ. Amen.

For the Nation's Families

O Lord Christ,
    by Your birth You brought
        God's love to the family of man;
    by Your sonship in a family at Nazareth
        You were obedient for us;
    by Your compassion for Mary and John
        at Your cross You revealed
        Your concern for the family.
We pray You, forgive in our nation's families
    our base sins of selfishness,
    our faithless sins of neglect,
    our unholy show of anger.
Keep our family members from
    impatience that destroys forgiveness,
    jealousy that hinders love,
    disobedience that mars unity.
Draw our family circles together
    by mutual forgiveness in Your name,
    by mutual love that comes from You,
    by mutual respect that reflects Your grace.
Hear us, that we may live as God's children
    made one by faith in You. Amen.

For Wisdom to Use Scientific Knowledge

Creator God, Maker of all things and Redeemer of man, we praise and thank You for the manner in which mysteries of the universe have been revealed to us. We are grateful for the legacy of science and all the benefits that it offers us. We count the accumulation of scientific knowledge as the sign of Your goodness and fatherly care for us. We see the expanse of the universe as the sign of Your infinite protection and care for us. We see in nuclear energy the sign of a power You have harnessed for our good.

We pray You therefore: Give us wisdom to use our scientific knowledge for the welfare of mankind. Turn what we have used for destructive purposes to beneficial goals. Direct what we know into useful and life-saving channels. Keep us from the folly of wasting our knowledge and resources on those things that advance only our egotism. Preserve us from the worship of science and the temptations of scientism. In Christ, who has set us free, give us the freedom to explore and learn, to experiment and serve with scientific precision to Your glory. Amen.

For Peace

Almighty God, Ruler of all things and all men:
    You hold the universe in Your palm,
    You have set all things to move in harmony,
    You desire that men dwell in unity and love.
We confess
    we have spoiled creation by our sin,
    we have disrupted harmony by our rebellion,
    we have divided our nation by selfishness.
We trust
    You will not permit sin to rule the day,
    You can bring order out of our confusion,
    You make nations instruments of Your will.
We implore You that You would
    crush men's lust for illicit power,
    stir in men respect for Your creation,
    kindle in men love for Your creatures.
To this end, we pray:
    raise up leaders everywhere who do Your will,
    make the nations obedient servants
        of Your purpose,
    teach men to live in service to one another.

Grant tranquillity, that the peace which the world cannot understand may be preached to the nations in the name of Your Son Jesus. Amen.

In Time of Prosperity

O Lord God, Creator of all things:
Accept our thanks
  for the prosperity You have given us,
  for the job opportunities to work and
    serve,
  for the gifts we have not deserved.
Remember Your children who hunger this
    day
  because of poverty,
  because of famine,
  because of war.
Forgive us for our failure
  to deal our bread to the hungry,
  to give to those who are needy,
  to share with those who want.
Help us and all men
  to devise new methods of distribution,
  to unscramble confused economies,
  to beat military hardware into plowshares.
Give to us
  love that knows no bounds,
  mercy that has no limits.
Teach us to see
  when we give to others, we give to You.
We ask it for the sake of Jesus,
  through whom You give all things. Amen.

In Time of War

Sovereign Lord, deal with us according to Your mercy. Forgive mankind for its inability to rise above the wrath and fury of war. Comfort all who mourn the losses of dear ones, who are homeless, and who are displaced by the violence of war. Prepare for death those who give themselves in sacrificial service. Stir men to valor and honor, but keep them humble and contrite. Raise up men who are able to bring peace out of our confusions. Restore order and justice where chaos and corruption must be overcome. Keep this war within the bounds of controllable limits. Hold men back from the futility of unleashing the full potential of nuclear war.

Above all, bring to a swift close this conflict. Cause the nations to resolve their differences by a mutual desire for equity. Hasten the day when men may return to useful tasks. If warfare continues, give us the vision to see Your will and to move swiftly to accomplish the same; through Christ, our Lord. Amen.

In Time of National Crisis
or Calamity

Heavenly Father, we cannot fathom the depth of meaning this crisis has for us now. We confess that as a people we have deserved to be visited with a heavy hand. We have worshiped too many gods. We have failed to honor Your name. We have turned deaf ears to Your Word. We have not upheld order and equity among men. We have been unchaste and impure.

Yet we pray You to hear our prayer for the sake of Your Son, our Lord. Have compassion and mercy. Set aside our guilt and give us new life through the merits of Your Son. Bring relief to all who suffer this day. Ease the anxieties of those who are distressed. Send help to those who are distraught. Release us from this fiery trial, that we may be free to give You thanks and glory for deliverance from the day of trouble. Amen.

For the Defense of Our Country

O blessed Lord, our Rock of Ages, we ask You to guard our nation constantly and to defend her especially in time of crisis. Because our enemies are many and powerful, we come to You to nullify their efforts. Preserve to our nation the blessings of prosperity and of religious freedom, and to us the Christian culture won by our forefathers at the cost of much personal sacrifice.

Help us that we, in appreciation of our national heritage and out of love for You, may transmit to our posterity the example of the life that is hid in Christ.

Should a national emergency arise, we implore You to come to our defense. Protect our homes and land from nuclear destruction and our shores from armed invasion. Grant that our nation never become involved in unprovoked wars, lest unjust loss of life and property inflicted on us and our enemies become a burden on conscience and bring men under Your judgment.

Help love and justice to prevail everywhere in our country, and grant that we ever seek Your will. In Jesus' name. Amen.

Memorial Day

Lord God, in whom there is life and light:
Accept
    our thanks for those who died for us,
    our prayers for those who mourn,
    our praise for the hope You have given us.
Refresh our hearts
    with dedication to the ideals of heroic
        men,
    with appreciation for the honesty of just
        men,
    with obedience to laws of upright men.
Forgive us
    when our patriotism is hollow,
    when our nationalism is arrogant,
    when our allegiance is halfhearted
Stir within us
    thanksgiving for all we have inherited,
    vigilance for the freedoms of all men,
    willingness to sacrifice for fellow citizens.
Comfort us with the joy that Christ
    died for all those who died for us,
    bringing life and immortality
    to light for all who believe in Him. Amen.

Independence Day

O Lord, we praise You
    that You have created us for freedom
        in Your creation,
    that You have re-created us for freedom
        under Your Gospel,
    that You enable us to keep Your law
        in freedom and love.
We confess
    we often neglect our rights,
    we often abuse our privileges,
    we often avoid our obligations.
Keep us
    from selfishness that stifles freedom,
    from narrow-mindedness that limits
        freedom,
    from hatred that destroys freedom.
Enable men everywhere
    to live under free government,
    to hear of the freedom of Your Gospel,
    to know true freedom in Jesus Christ,
        our Lord, in whose name we ask it.
        Amen.

Labor Day

Lord God, our Father and Creator:
We deserve
    to labor among thorns and thistles,
    to eat by the sweat of our brow,
    to work without reward,
For we confess
    we have spoiled Your creation by our sin,
    we have marred our work by our neglect,
    we have hurt Your work by our rebellion.
We pray You, bless our labor
    by Him who was once a carpenter,
    by Him who came to be our servant,
    by Him who saved us to serve.
For His sake keep us and all who labor
    from false dealing and unfair practice,
    from excessive profit and unjust gain,
    from slovenly service and irrational
        demands.
Help us
    to labor with love,
    to labor with joy,
    to labor with faithfulness.
Teach us that the best labor we give You
    is loving service to our fellowmen.
In Christ's name we ask it. Amen.

Thanksgiving Day

Heavenly Father,
> from whom come all good and perfect gifts,
> from whom come mercies new each day,
> from whom come blessings beyond measure:

Accept our thanksgiving
> for protection and those who provide it,
> for daily bread and those who prepare it,
> for clothing and those who manufacture it,
> for family and those dear to us,
> for friends and those associated with us,
> for jobs and those working with us,
> for social security and support programs.

We confess we think too little
> about the fact that we deserve nothing,
> about the many who serve us,
> about the blessings of Your Spirit.

We pray You,
> forgive our ingratitude,
> open our eyes to behold Your goodness,
> fill our hearts with thankfulness,
> make us respond in appreciation,
> help us to serve in love.

We thank You; through Christ, our Lord,
> Your best gift to us. Amen.

PRAYERS
FOR
OTHERS

For Those Who Work
in the Medical Arts

We come before You now, O God, with the knowledge that You have created us and are also able to restore us. Because You are the Great Physician, we pray for those whom You use to perform Your works of healing. We rejoice that Your Spirit leads men and women to become doctors, nurses, dentists, research scientists, medical technicians, orderlies, and hospital staff members. We thank and praise You for the miracles You perform through them.

Dear God, keep our minds open to new truths concerning the cause and cure of disease. Help us to realize that our talents and knowledge are gifts from You, to be used to serve all men. Most of all, we ask You to fill the hearts of medical staff people everywhere with Your love, Your patience, and Your compassion.

We especially ask Your blessing upon _____ in their life of service to You and mankind. Draw them closer to Your Son Jesus as their Lord, their Guide, and their Savior. In His name we pray. Amen.

For Those Who Work in the Fine Arts

We thank You, heavenly Father! What else can we say when we consider the uplifting contributions that artists have added to our lives through canvas, sculpture, stage, pen, and music? Life would be drab and dull without them. We would be depressed by the ugly, the sad, the chaotic, and the complex in life were it not for them. We ask You to guide the brush, the knife, the chisel, the hammer, or whatever other instruments are used to create works of art.

Keep the efforts of artists from becoming an escape from life. Let their art express the height and the depth, the length and the breadth of the world as You would have them see it. Open our minds to understand the world better through their creations. May those employing canvas, stone, metal, wood, spoken and written words, staff, notes, and chords express life in its best and noblest form. We ask You to inspire artists with a faith that will give us a new vision of Your glory. In Jesus' name. Amen.

For Those Who Work in Science

O God, we pray for men of science who serve in laboratories, whose lives are engaged with tubes, microscopes, reactors, and instruments, and whose world is one of theories and laws, of dreams and frustrations.

We confess that at times we become disturbed by the changes their research produces in our lives. Forgive us if through ignorance or a false sense of loyalty to Your creative power we criticize their efforts or minimize their achievements. Lead us to appreciate more fully the vast new world of knowledge, technique, service, and healing that science has opened for us under Your divine guidance and benediction.

Help us understand that You use these men and women of science to reveal truths about Yourself, Your world, and us. Grant to them vision to see not only the vastness and complexity of creation but also the Creator. Give them the wisdom and freedom in Christ to use their discoveries for the service of mankind and to Your glory. We ask this in the name of Jesus, who is eternal Truth. Amen.

For Those Who Work in Education

O great and eternal God, whose wisdom all creation declares and history exalts, grant guidance and help to those teaching on all levels of learning. You have charged them with the responsibility of passing on to each generation the wisdom of the past, the discoveries of the present, and the hope of the future. Grant them understanding that they may see each student as an individual, with a body, mind, and soul redeemed by Christ.

Help them to use their profession wisely to stimulate thought rather than to stifle it; to challenge initiative rather than to discourage it; to encourage effort rather than to frustrate it. Give to boards of education on all levels a sense of vision and concern that rises above petty politics or personalities.

Above all, O Lord, keep those who are leaders in the field of education mindful that their own lives reflect the greatest lesson they can teach. May those who have seen Jesus live their convictions and lead others to true wisdom. We ask this in the name of Him who is the Truth. Amen.

For Those Who Work in the Performing Arts

Forgive us, dear heavenly Father, if in our prayer for those engaged in the performing arts we recall with a smile the humor and spice they add to life. It would indeed be a dull world without them. In bestowing gifts and talents to men, You have thought of all our needs. Certainly in the rush and struggle of daily living we need time to leave our burdens and cares behind and to let our imaginations soar to the beauty of song and dance and music; to laugh at ourselves in the amusing antics and routines of comics; and to let our minds identify with others through radio, television, stage, and screen.

Thank You, Father, for the people who serve us in these fields. Give those seeking careers in these vocations an extra measure of courage, patience, and persistence. Remind those who have reached the plateau of success that their abilities have come from You. And convince all that their lives should be a witness to You.

We ask You to bestow a special measure of blessing upon our favorite entertainers. Hear us for the sake of Jesus. Amen.

For Those Who Work in Industry

Lord God, Source of every blessing, we thank You for the prosperity our nation enjoys above all others on earth. Without Your gifts of natural resources and mineral deposits and the processes of automation and technology we would still be a poor, backward people.

O Lord, we praise You for having crowned with success the programs devised by our leaders in industry, finance, and business. Amidst our affluence keep us humble. Make us a truly grateful people. Help all those who are engaged in business to see You as the One ultimately responsible for the wealth and prosperity we enjoy.

Continue to bless us as a nation. Lead both employer and employee to recognize their common needs and contributions. Cause harmony and peace to prevail in all walks of public life. Preserve us from dethroning You and enthroning profit instead as our god. Help us in the midst of prosperity to retain a balanced sense of values, a spirit of service to all, and the readiness to walk in the footsteps of Christ, who went about doing good. For Jesus' sake. Amen.

For Those Who Work in Agriculture

Lord of the harvest, we thank You for the richness of our soil that causes crops to abound beyond the needs of our country. Our bounty is so vast that our government curtails the production of certain foods lest they glut the market. Your generosity exceeds our grasp.

We ask You to continue to bless the efforts of those who till the soil. Prosper the work of those engaged in agricultural research to increase the produce of the earth. Give dignity to common toil.

Help those who work with nature to see You reflected there. When rain and sunshine seemingly do not come in proper amounts and crops suffer, remind agricultural workers that the powers of nature are ever in Your hand and that all things occur to accomplish Your will. Spare them discouragement. Give them faith to trust that Your ways are best even though we cannot understand them.

And as they engage in the production of daily bread for the body, remind them to seek the Bread of life daily for their immortal souls; through Christ Jesus. Amen.

For Those Who Serve
Where We Cannot Be

Almighty and allwise God, this universe is too vast, and our lives too complicated, for our puny intellects to grasp. We thank You for the infinite love and providence that have marvelously fashioned us and all things.

In Your divine governance You involve untold thousands in the manufacture and production of the supplies that provide for the needs of all mankind. For all these invisible and unknown contributors to our daily welfare we give You hearty thanks. We ask that You bless them in their work. Enlarge their vision that they view their employment not just as a job but as a service to others and as an act whereby they worship You. Grant them the satisfaction of work well done. Give them the spirit of honesty, integrity, faithfulness, unselfishness, cooperation, and joy. Enable them to see themselves as the interrelated persons of a vast human society, each with a task to perform that serves the welfare of all. Above all, O Lord, engage them for Your service through a living faith in Jesus. Amen.

For Those Who Mourn

Almighty and eternal God, in whose hands are life and death, we come into Your presence to plead for all who mourn. Even as Your Son was moved to weep over the death of His friend Lazarus, so we know that You are touched by the tears of those who grieve over the loss of dear ones. In Your divine providence fill the aching void in their hearts with Your comforting presence, and wipe all tears from their eyes.

Source of all consolation, raise them up with the hope in Christ. Reassure them of an eternal reunion in Your presence with their beloved, whom You have called to eternal peace and immeasurable joy in heaven. In their loneliness draw them closer to You.

O Lord, cause the sorrow of separation to make the survivors more understanding of the grief of others and more ready to comfort them in their needs.

We ask this in the name of Jesus, who died that we might live forever. Amen.

For Those in Military Service

Dear heavenly Father, our hearts are in distress when we think of the many young men of our land who are called into military service to defend their country at great personal sacrifice, sometimes contrary to their own convictions. Keep them from becoming bitter or discouraged. Help them realize that Your divine providence always controls their lives and that, come what may, all things will work together for their ultimate good.

Grant them courage to perform their duties well. Keep their minds and bodies pure. Shield them from harm and temptation. In doubts and fears give them a conquering faith. Enable them ever so to live and to serve that they will be Your effectual witnesses.

Dear Lord, soon end all strife and establish peace among the people of the earth. Meanwhile we entrust our loved ones to Your guidance and care. In Jesus' name. Amen.

For Those in Combat

Gracious God and Father, we come before You pleading for those who are fighting on our behalf. They too are Your children. Watch over them with Your all-seeing eye and protect them with Your almighty power.

As they go into battle or are engaged in combat, give them strength and courage to face each crisis, relying on Your providential care. Through each trying experience draw them closer to You. In moments of desperation help them find the calm assurance of Your presence.

Should You require some unusual task or an extraordinary sacrifice of them, give them readiness to respond cheerfully to Your will. Increase their faith in the midst of adversity. In every emergency lead them to cast all their care upon You. Heal them when wounded, comfort them when suffering, and sustain them when dying. Above all, keep them in such intimate contact with You that, living or dying, they may remain Yours. This we ask in Jesus' name. Amen.

For the Unemployed

We thank You, Lord God, for the physical, intellectual, and spiritual endowments with which You have equipped us for the privilege of serving with them. But, O Lord, there are many who because of handicaps are unemployable, or because of economic dislocations have no work or only part-time employment. We ask You to take them into Your divine care and keeping. Assure them of Your love and favor. Although deprived of the dignity of common toil, remind them that they are human beings with as much dignity before You as the greatest of men.

To all who cannot work give a sense of fulfillment in serving with the leisure time they have as a result of their unemployment. Do not allow them or their families to suffer want or privation. In due time grant them again gainful employment. Whether they are employed or unemployed, preserve their sense of dignity and self-respect as humans, and give them the conviction that in their place they are making a contribution to society and to You as their Creator and Lord. For Jesus' sake. Amen.

For the Poor and Hungry

Almighty and gracious God, in our abundance it is difficult for us to realize that many people are hungry. The earth You have created can bring forth food for all, but because of selfishness, thoughtlessness, and other reasons some lack daily bread. So often we have not concerned ourselves with the welfare of our neighbors. Forgive us our sins of indifference, neglect, coldness, and lovelessness.

Look in mercy on the poor and hungry in their suffering, and supply their wants. Keep them from becoming discouraged, bitter, and resentful. Ever be their refuge in time of affliction, and cause them to experience Your infinite love and power.

Help us to see the needs of the people on our street, in our community, and throughout the world. Kindle in our hearts a love that radiates sympathy, kindness, concern, and generosity to all mankind.

We thank You for our many blessings. Help us to share them with the poor, hungry, and underprivileged. Above all, make us ready to share with them Your Son, in whose name we pray. Amen.

For Minorities

O righteous and eternal God, You have called us to do justice and to love mercy. As citizens of a country dedicated to freedom for minorities, we pray for greater human justice to all men, and a deeper understanding of the problems that beset them. As more and more people crowd into our cities, with their social diversities and problems of transiency, grant all men love for one another as persons whom You have created. Deepen in us concern for the appalling conditions of city ghettos, sympathy for the needs of the poverty-stricken and underprivileged, and patience with others in all walks of life. Move us to work for the removal of the evils that trouble minority groups, so that a truly unified society may emerge in which justice and order may prevail.

Meanwhile grant all men the spirit of self-restraint that will discourage violence and disobedience to the laws of the land. Banish all greed, selfishness, and prejudice. Instead establish peace, harmony, love, and goodwill in the spirit of Your Son. Amen.

For All Travelers

Almighty and ever-present God, we ask You to watch over those who are today traveling by land, sea, or air. We thank You for our modern transportation. Bless all efforts to insure safe travel. Make the technicians who produce and service the various vehicles of transit conscientious and careful.

Give pilots of planes alert minds and steady nerves. Guide them and their passengers safely to their destination.

On our highways help the operators of cars, trucks, and buses observe the laws enacted for their safety. Keep them from becoming reckless, careless, sleepy, or ill while driving.

On the railways of the world grant guidance and alertness to all engineers and firemen, and faithfulness and concern to all train crews.

Protect men everywhere on their travels. Should accidents occur, give comfort to the injured, calm to the confused, and peace to the dying. Above all, help travelers ever to be ready to meet You at journey's end. In the name of Jesus, who is our Way. Amen.

For the Mentally Ill

Lord God, in the days of His flesh Your Son went about doing good, driving out demons from the possessed, and helping the mentally deranged. We ask You to bless the ministries performed for those similarly afflicted in our age. Grant guidance, insight, and success to all who are engaged in research in mental illness. Cause the prescribed medication, treatment, and surgery to help those afflicted with mental and nervous disorders.

Relieve all distressed patients from a sense of guilt or depression, and show them that there is forgiveness in the blood of Christ. Remind them that Jesus is the Friend especially of sinners and the afflicted. Comfort them with the knowledge that their Lord loves them with an everlasting love and that, though He has permitted this affliction to come upon them, He will sustain them with His grace. Help them to sense Your divine presence, even though they be in confinement. Always assure them that underneath are the everlasting arms of their Lord. For the sake of Jesus. Amen.

For Those Trapped in Sinful Habits

Almighty and eternal God, though You have made man as the crowning masterpiece of Your creation only to see him through sin fall into misery and degradation, we ask You to have mercy on those who through their own irresponsibility or the guile and greed of others have fallen victim to sinful habits.

Lord, grant them superhuman strength to extricate themselves from the tenacious grip of vicious habits. Help them to see that all things are possible for them through Christ, who strengthens them.

In Your mercy shift their devotion from things material to the spiritual concerns of the life in Christ. Remind them that their bodies are the temple of Your Holy Spirit and that one day they must give an account of their present abuse.

Help them to discover that there is forgiveness in the blood of Jesus, reinstatement as Your beloved children by faith in the Savior, and the hope of eternal glory in the cross of their Redeemer. For the sake of Jesus, who died to remove sin. Amen.

For the Lonely

Dear heavenly Father, since in infinite love for fallen mankind You sent Your Son to redeem us from all evil, we can be free from the evil of loneliness inasmuch as Jesus suffered loneliness for us in Gethsemane and on Calvary. Yet many of Your children are still lonely today, and we pray You to be with them, O Lord. Fill their hearts with a sense of Your divine presence; then there will be no room for loneliness. If they are separated from family and friends, may they remember that You as their heavenly Father hold them together in Your loving care. Assure them that since they are members of the body of Christ their prayers unite at Your throne with the prayers of their beloved, even though they and their family are miles apart.

If selfishness contributes to the loneliness of Your children, help them to forget themselves in the service of others and thus find purpose and fulfillment in their lives. As they rededicate themselves to You, grant that they may never feel alone again. In the name of Jesus, our Friend and Companion. Amen.

For Prisoners

Dear loving Lord, who at the Great Judgment will commend the faithful: "I was in prison, and you came to Me," we plead for those behind prison walls.

Regardless of what may have brought them to this place in life, look upon them with Your profound mercy, and lead them to experience Your infinite love. Help them to realize that they are not alone in their guilt, for all have sinned and come short of the glory of God. Show them that because of Your limitless grace they are not too evil to come to You for forgiveness and help, for guidance and comfort, for strength and renewal.

Keep them from bitterness or hatred toward their fellowmen. Help them to begin a new life centered in You.

Finally, cause us to do all we can to reclaim for the heavenly kingdom those who according to men's standards may have committed greater sins than we, but who according to Your standards are just as precious as any of Your children. In Your mercy hear us. Amen.

For the Sick

Dear Lord Jesus, when You walked upon this earth, You healed the sick, gave sight to the blind, caused the lame to walk, and raised the dead. Now we come to You in behalf of those who are suffering today and pray that You would send them Your healing power.

Dearest Lord, You have suffered all things. You know and understand their pain. We ask You to ease their suffering, to quiet their fears, and to direct their eyes to Your cross. Grant them penitent hearts and by Your grace forgive their sins. As they lie on their beds of pain, help them look beyond the ceiling of their room to Your throne in the heavens. Take their hand in Yours that they may receive that peace which You alone can give. Since the holy Word promises that "in everything God works for good with those who love Him," teach them confidently to place themselves into Your gracious care, saying, "Not my will but Yours be done."

Hear our prayer for Your name's sake. Amen.

For the Children and Youth

Dear heavenly Father, we entrust our children and youth to Your allwise and loving care. You have given them to us as a sacred charge. Help us to rear them with patience, firmness, and love. Make our children strong in body and mind. Preserve them from accidents and sicknesses. Cause them to feel secure in Your tender love. Keep them free from fears and anxieties.

Enable them to grow up to be sincere, honest, obedient, considerate, kind, and useful disciples of Jesus. In their activities make them helpful to those round about them by developing and sharing the talents You have given them. Help them not to be jealous of others. Make them aware of the many things You have given them. May they always give first place to Your glory and to the welfare of others.

Above all, give them a strong faith. Lead them to know the joy of Your salvation as they come to You daily in prayer for forgiveness, help, guidance, and inspiration. Ever keep them close to You as Your loving children, redeemed by the blood of Your Son and their Savior. Amen.

For the Aged

Gracious heavenly Father, You sustain us day by day. Even in the golden years of life You richly bless us. For this we thank You. Yet our hearts are troubled when we think of the growing number of aged today. Many of them appear to be neglected and forgotten as they spend the evening of their lives in hospitals, nursing homes, and homes for the aged. Many are in pain. Others have financial worries. Loneliness grips many. Assure them: "Lo, I am with you always."

You know and understand their problems better than we. Help us to see and alleviate their difficulties. Keep these aging people in Your tender care. Forgive them their doubts, fears, and anxieties.

Lord, light with faith
    their morning road,
Walk close to them today,
And grant Your true and lasting peace
To them along the way.
Lord, fill with strength
    their evening road,
And when the day is through
Give them Your solace and Your grace,
And guide their steps to You. Amen.

PRAYERS
FOR
INDIVIDUAL AND FAMILY
OCCASIONS

Wedding Day

Lord God, heavenly Father, we thank You for our wedding day. You have created man and woman to live together to Your glory and for their welfare. We thank You for having brought us together as husband and wife. Grant that our love always be rooted in that greater love given us in Your Son Jesus Christ, our Lord. We ask for a full measure of the Holy Spirit's wisdom to direct us in all we think, say, and do, and to help us solve the problems that arise in marital life.

Give us physical, mental, and spiritual health for a useful and happy life. Grant us success in our daily work. When trials and tensions come, sustain us. Help us always to have the grace to forgive each other's sins, to correct misunderstandings, and to forgive failures, even as *our* sins are forgiven by You for Jesus' sake.

We pray also that others may see in our lives the joy of a Christian heart and home. Keep us faithful to Your Word and constant in prayer. We have taken our vows in Your name, O triune God. Therefore, Lord, bless us and be present in our home always. Amen.

Wedding Anniversary

Dear Father in heaven, on this anniversary of our marriage we thank You for the grace, mercy, and goodness You have given us in Christ, our Lord. We confess that at times we were sinful and selfish. We hurt each other, our loved ones about us, and You by our sin. We did not always show that perfect love which is in Christ. But You forgave us for Jesus' sake. By the renewal of Your Spirit we grew stronger in faith, in our responsibilities as husband and wife, and in service to each other and our family. For this we thank You, O Lord.

Marriage is Your creation for the welfare of man. Keep it sacred in our day. Use us to show others that man and woman find their highest happiness in Christ.

As we move on together in life, we are confident of Your continued blessings. We remember gratefully that in the past Your Word sustained us in days of anxiety and trial and gave us many happy days to enjoy. Fill us now with Your Spirit. Increase our love for You and for each other. Strengthen our faith and continue to bless us in work and service for You; through Christ. Amen.

Birth of a Child

We thank You, dear Lord, for blessing our life with the gift of a newborn child. Our love for You and each other deepens, and we find ourselves unable to express in words the feeling of closeness that this new child brings into our life. In this day when men expect so many marvelous things through study and discovery, we recognize that the conception and birth of a child are evidence of Your creative power and goodness.

Bless our child with a healthy body and a good mind. As we bring our child to You in the washing of Holy Baptism, we believe that You will give him (her) the new birth into Your family in which we all are members by Your grace through Christ, our Redeemer. May our child grow up in Your favor and in service to all men. Give us the necessary health, wisdom, and strength to rear our child according to Your Word. Bless us as a family through Christ, our Lord, the Savior of all men, and the Friend of children. Amen.

Baptism of a Child

Dear Lord, at Your gracious invitation we are bringing our child to You in Holy Baptism. We thank You that in this sacrament You give it new birth and life, making it a member of Your holy family. As our child grows up, the world will often appear strange, challenging, and confusing. We realize that temptation and trial will come to it in many forms and ways. For such times especially keep our child in its baptismal grace.

On this day we also recall with gratitude our own baptism. Remind us again that we begin, live out, and conclude each day of our life as members of Your heavenly household. Help us to live in this world as Your redeemed children, serving You and our fellowmen in love and devotion. In doing so we praise Your holy name, O blessed Trinity. Amen.

Confirmation of a Child

This day brings joy into our hearts and home, dear Lord. We thank You for the covenant You made with us and our children in Holy Baptism. You have brought our son (daughter) through the study of Your Word to know the meaning of his (her) baptism, to stand before the world and confess Your name as the only true God, in whom we have life eternal. You have blessed us with a Christian home. For all of this we thank You. We are grateful also for our church, our congregation, the pastor, and the teachers who have helped us in teaching our child Your Word. We are thankful likewise for the sponsors who have assisted us in our responsibility.

Equip us all our days for the demands of a bold and constant Christian witness. Renew us each day, along with our child, in our baptismal grace, so that we honor Your holy name and praise it forever, O Holy Trinity. Amen.

Confirmation Day

You have led me, O God, to this day of my confirmation. I have been taught the meaning of my baptism, in which I was brought to You as a child. My parents, teachers, and pastor have given me guidance and help in learning Your way of life. And now I thank You that I can stand before this Christian congregation today and with my own lips confess my faith in You. I want to be Your child forever. I have looked forward to this day for a long time.

As I pledge loyalty to You, I ask that Your Holy Spirit would keep me in my baptismal grace for the days ahead. Help me to serve You and my fellowman faithfully. Remind me that I grow in Your favor as I use Your Word daily and apply it to my life. Lead me to honor You, my parents, my family, and my church through a life of selfless service.

Finally crown my faith in You with heavenly glory; through Jesus Christ, my Savior and Lord. Amen.

Graduation

Dear Lord, You have brought me to this goal of my formal education. Today as I receive my diploma I thank You for the support of my parents during the past, for my teachers, and for all who helped me along the way. Although I began my schooling with high ideals, I was often overwhelmed by the volume of materials and subject matter of the courses. Sometimes I felt that I was not allowed to think for myself. Plans were made for me by my parents and teachers. Society with its demands, and people by their words and actions, confused me.

I confess also that there were days when my faith and my confidence in You were shaken. But Your Word was my guide and help. Through it Your Holy Spirit stabilized me and gave me the faith, strength, and ability to carry on and to reach the goal of graduation. For all this I thank You, O Lord.

And now as I face the future, grant me a keen sense of responsibility and calling in life. Assure me again of Your guidance and blessing for the days ahead. In all that I do, O God, help me to glorify Your name; through Christ, my Lord. Amen.

Expectant Mother

O Lord, Creator of all life, I am filled with wonder at the mystery of human conception and birth. I thank You for this gift of pregnancy. Grant me health for the days ahead. Give to this child within me a strong body and a sound mind. Keep me mindful of my role as a wife and mother. Increase my love for You and for my husband. Keep us both strong in our faith in You as our Savior and Redeemer, and help us share our love and affection for each other in mutual helpfulness and service.

May we reveal to others the joy of a Christ-centered life. Help us praise Your name for the creative power of Your presence in our home, evidenced by the gift of a child. Give a normal birth to our expected infant. We look forward to its birth also into the kingdom of Your grace through Holy Baptism. I thank You, Lord, in Jesus' name for blessing me in this miraculous way. Amen.

Mother

Dear Lord, I am grateful for the gift of motherhood. I do confess, however, that my many duties and cares for my family often leave me weary and worn out at the end of the day. At times I become irritable and fretful. I do not seem to have sufficient time for rest and for the relaxed association a mother needs with her husband and family.

Give me the strength and health required to perform all of my obligations as a Christian mother. Fill me with deep affection for my husband and children. Grant our family Your Holy Spirit, so that we grow together from day to day in Your love and that we order and shape our lives with wisdom according to Your will. Make me a worthy example of a Christian mother, and let many see in our home the joy of a family in which father, mother, and children dwell together in Christ.

Continue to assure me of Your grace through Christ, my Lord and Savior, who honored His mother in the very hour in which He gave His life on the cross for me and all men. Thank You, Lord, for the gift of children and motherhood. Amen.

Father

By the mystery of Your wisdom and grace, O Lord, I am a father. You have given my wife and me the blessings of a Christian marriage and home. For this and for the gift of our children we thank You. Give me the strength to set an example of the joy and privilege of fatherhood. Help me so to arrange my busy schedule, with all its demanding pressures, that I may devote myself to my loved ones and we as a family find sufficient time to work, pray, and play together. I confess that I have often failed You in the past in my role as a father. For the sake of Jesus, forgive my sins.

Give me courage to follow Your will when I am tried and torn by the tensions and temptations common to my occupation and position. Grant me the wisdom to lead my family in the regular use of Your holy Word and sacraments — the means You have supplied for our growth in faith, life, and service. Bless my daily work, and provide us with all we need for our physical and temporal wants. Give us all health of body, mind, and soul. By Your power help us walk the road to heaven together; for Jesus' sake. Amen.

Sponsor

Lord God, since I have been asked by Christian parents to serve as a sponsor for their child, make me fully aware of the importance of this trust. Let me understand the seriousness of the obligation I am assuming to assist the parents in the Christian training of their child. Help me to discharge this responsibility humbly and faithfully in the strength of Your Spirit received in my own baptism.

By Your nurture and care in my daily life, make me an example of Christian devotion to this child, and help me to assist in teaching it the meaning of Holy Baptism in Your name. As it grows older, enable this child, along with all of us who have received the new birth through the water of Baptism, to begin each day in the assurance of sins forgiven. Give it power to walk in the way of Christ.

In company with the whole Christian church on earth we continually praise You for the gift of this sacrament of Holy Baptism and hold its gracious use sacred to the glory of Your name, O Holy Trinity, the Father and the Son and the Holy Spirit. Amen.

Catechumen

Gracious God, I thank You for the opportunity to attend classes for a more thorough study of Your Word. Such instruction is the gift of Your pure mercy. Enable me to appreciate this privilege fully and to apply myself faithfully to the study of these lessons. Enlighten my understanding by Your Holy Spirit. Teach me the profound meaning of my baptism, and lead me to a stronger faith.

I thank You for the faithful pastors and teachers who lead me and my classmates in Your way. We are gathered as members of Your family by the action of Your Spirit. Oh, keep us close to You and to one another by the power of Your holy Gospel! Help us to hear and learn Your Word gladly, so that we may know the joy of a Christian life.

If at times we become frustrated in the course of our studies, strengthen and encourage us through Your Holy Spirit. Bless us always for the sake of Jesus, our Savior. Amen.

Student

Lord God, heavenly Father, I recognize the need for a thorough education today. The opportunities for study seem almost limitless. As a Christian I realize that I am to use all my gifts for the glory of Your name and the welfare of man. I must confess that many times in the daily course of study the pressures become wearying. Often I am confused by the many views I hear and read about. The swift changes in the realm of thought are frequently bewildering. My Christian faith often is shaken.

But I remember, O Christ, that You are eternal Wisdom. In days of academic stress and strain, I pray, stabilize me by Your Word and presence. Grant that I apply myself to my studies with diligence and zeal. Help me to grow in depth of understanding and to employ the tools of learning effectively in my calling in life. Enable me to see Your creative and saving hand in all things. Show me how to witness to the joy of my Christian faith and to the wholeness of one who is filled with Christian concern. Give meaning and purpose to all that I think and do; for Jesus' sake. Amen.

Student of Theology

Eternal God, Lord of the church, since our world is in desperate need of men to explore the Sacred Scriptures and to lay Your Word with clarity and conviction before others, give us many young people who will prepare for full-time service in Your church.

I thank You that You have privileged me to engage in the study of theology. Give me a continuous, urgent sense of calling for the holy ministry. Grant me energy and zeal to pursue my studies diligently in the various disciplines of my chosen vocation. As I work with the Sacred Scriptures, remove my doubts, strengthen my faith, and inspire me for a life of dedicated service. By Your Holy Spirit bring the needs of men into clear focus for me.

In the days ahead equip me with a clear and incisive mind for my work. Make me flexible and adaptable to the changing moods and conditions of the world. Keep me firmly grounded and rooted in Christ in all that I think, write, say, and do. Take me and use me, O Lord, to reveal Your Word to others. In Your name I pray. Amen.

Widow or Widower

O Lord, I am lonely and at times I feel forsaken. Forgive me, for I know You are with me always. Strengthen my faith by Your Spirit. Give me the comfort and assurance of the many promises in Your Word. In days of sorrow and heartache, as well as in times of joy and happiness, You are always present.

Help me to be grateful for the years my spouse and I shared happily in this world. When I am tempted to pity myself, to complain, and even to rebel against my present lot, by Your Holy Spirit make me remember that all that I have has come from Your undeserved mercy. As Your child in Christ I am assured of Your constant love and concern.

Hold before me the victory over the grave which we all have in You, who rose from the dead and live as the victor over sin, death, and hell. Keep me busy in the service of others. May they see in me the courage and joy of Christian faith. I praise Your holy name now and forever, O Lord. Amen.

Single Adult

At present, dear Lord, it appears to be Your will for me, along with many others in society, to live a single life. Help me, as one who is not married, to appreciate Your creation of the family. Let me find my responsibility and role in serving the families of others in society. Give me a keen sense of concern for my fellowman.

By my example of Christian faith and devotion lead others to see the purposeful place of the single person in the community and family. Keep me healthy and happy in my views of marriage. If it is Your will that in time I find a partner, grant a happy and blessed marriage that will glorify Your name.

Meanwhile accomplish Your good and gracious will in me. Never permit me to be withdrawn and selfish in the company of others. Remind me of Your constant companionship. And cause me always, together with my relatives and friends, to sing Your praises, O God, from whom we receive life and health and every good. In Jesus' name I ask it. Amen.

One Who Is Divorced

Heavenly Father, I know that separation and divorce are the result of sin. Forgive me for my failure in marriage. Do not permit me to become bitter. Help me to witness to men that I believe marriage is a holy relationship which You have created.

From the depths of a truly penitent heart I pray for a godly life that will be an example to others. Keep me humble, and give me contentment as I serve others in Christian love. Grant my former mate Your forgiveness and a happy and blessed life. Whatever the future holds in store for us, bestow Your divine benediction upon all our activities.

I pray also for all married couples facing temptations and problems that are often too great for human strength and intelligence. Satan desires to destroy us and our families. Grant relief, O Lord, from the evil of divorce, and restore the family to its hallowed place in society. Rule our hearts and homes by Your love, and fill the days ahead with Your presence, O Holy Trinity. Amen.

Mourners

Lord, we mourn the death of our dear one. Our loss makes us lonely, at times critical, and sometimes even rebellious against You. Forgive us our sins. Increase our faith in Christ, who is the Resurrection and the Life. As the wages of sin is death, so Your gift is eternal life through the life, death, and resurrection of Your Son, our Savior.

By Your mercy make our dying here become our entrance to life eternal with You. Since we are members of the body of Christ, we are certain that when we leave this world we will be reunited with our loved one in Your presence in heavenly joy. Give us the ability to reflect this conviction in our lives.

O Holy Spirit, You are our Strength and Comforter. Give us courage to carry on in our daily vocation. Keep us active in helping others. Supply all our needs of body and soul. Give us a faith that radiates joy and hope. We pray in Your name, O God, in whom we live and move and have our being. Amen.

Those Engaged

Lord of love, we are grateful that our love has grown and deepened so that now we are planning marriage. We look forward to living together as husband and wife. Give us Your wisdom and counsel as we plan our wedding and our home. Keep us in our baptismal grace, and grant that our love always remain built upon Your greater love for us as our Savior and God.

Remind us that as Your children we belong body and soul to You. Give us each day the power to respond to Your will in thought, word, and deed. Cultivate within us constant respect and concern for each other. Help us to experience Your grace and love in a long and happy married life together. In Your name we pray, O Lord Christ. Amen.

The Traveler

Lord, as I join the host of travelers, I am conscious of the constant danger of accident, injury, and death. Guard and protect me on my way. Send Your holy angels to be with me and with my fellow travelers that no harm may come to us. Grant success to all my undertakings. Give me the grace to pause along the way to refresh my soul in worship.

Help me to be concerned about the welfare of others traveling by land, sea, or air. Cause my absence from loved ones to lead me to a greater appreciation of home and family. Whether we are together or apart, remind us that we are always together in Your care and protection.

I commend myself and all travelers into Your hands, through Christ, my Lord, who came into this world to lead us all on the journey of life to our eternal dwelling place with Him in heaven. Amen.

The Retired

Dear Lord, I heartily thank You for the years of my life. They have been rich in blessing. In good and evil times Your hand sustained me. Continue to lead me, O God.

Now that I am free from a daily schedule of work, help me to seize every opportunity to witness to Your love and presence. Keep me interested in those about me, lest I become bored and frustrated. Give me health, ability, and readiness to continue to work in Your church. Enable me to contribute the common sense, understanding, and judgment I have acquired through my experience in life.

May Your Spirit give me strength and determination to do those things for You now which I was unable to do in former years because of my employment. Let others in retirement see from my example that true Christians can be useful all the days of their life here on earth. And finally bring us all to our heavenly home. This I ask for the sake of Christ, my Lord. Amen.

On Facing Military Service

Lord, as I am about to enter the military service of my country, lead me to understand and accept this assignment as Your will for my life. Inspire me with a true sense of duty to defend my countrymen. Grant me always the certainty of Your presence and the assurance of Your protection. Give me the power of the Holy Spirit to conduct myself according to Your will in every situation.

Bless me, O Father, with contentment, patience, courage, and commitment to my mission. Bring me safely through this period of military service, and by this experience lead me to grow in spirit and in favor with You and my fellowmen. Upon the completion of my military career return me safely to civilian life, matured in body, mind, and soul, and allow me many more days and years to serve You.

I commend myself into Your hands with confidence, trusting that all things work together for good to those who love You. I am Yours always, O heavenly Father, and Christ is mine by the gift of the Holy Spirit. I thank You heartily for the promises Your Word offers me in Christ, my Lord. Amen.

One in Military Service

My changed life under the discipline of military service is often hard to understand, Lord God. At times I am upset and confused by my orders and directives. Sometimes they seem to make no sense to me. The waiting and the anxiety frequently try my nerves. Temptations of every kind confront me.

Enable me, O Lord, to wear the uniform of my country with dignity and honor, revealing at all times to those about me the confidence I have in Your Word. Give me the courage to use every opportunity to witness to my faith in You, my Lord and Savior. Lead me through every act of my daily schedule to show my superiors and associates the blessings of a life committed to You. Give me wisdom to choose what is right and to avoid what is evil.

Increase my faith in Your gracious will for me and for all men in Christ. Forgive me when I fail in my duty and sin against You and others. Strengthen my trust in Your Word of promise, and make it my constant companion and guide. In Jesus' name I pray. Amen.

One in Combat

Dear Lord, I have received my orders for combat duty. Fear and anxiety upset me. I hesitate to injure or kill any of my fellowmen. In this crisis of my life assure me especially of Your presence, guidance, and protection. If it be Your will, do not place me in a position where I must harm anyone or be hurt myself.

Have mercy on all men. Put an end to war and violence everywhere. Speedily persuade the leaders of all who are engaged in this conflict to come to the peace table. If it be Your will, bring me home again to my loved ones, safe and sound, healthy in body and spirit. Grant me many happy days ahead with my family. Help me to dedicate myself in the future to the promotion of peace and goodwill among men.

Meanwhile, O God, I commend myself, my body and soul, and all things to You, whose own I have become in baptism. Command Your holy angels to be with me now. By Your Holy Spirit strengthen my confidence that I shall always remain Yours through Christ, my Lord, whom You sent into this world to bring peace. Amen.

Family Moving
to a New Community

Heavenly Father, guide and direct us as we break our community ties and leave friends and neighbors to move into a new locality. Assure us that this change is for our good and for the welfare of many. Help us always to cherish our longtime friends and also to welcome new ones.

Make this change in environment and association another opportunity to witness to our Christian faith. Lead those about us to see the tie that binds our family together in the love of Jesus, our Lord. Give us the ability to radiate Christian warmth and courtesy in our new community. Enable us to set an example of devotion to duty in our church and home, and make us equal to civic responsibility in our community.

Bless us with health of body, soul, and mind. Dwell in our hearts and make us a happy family no matter where our home may be; for Jesus' sake. Amen.

For the Family at Home

Lord, when I think of my family members from whom I am separated, my heart is heavy and I am lonely. I learn to appreciate more fully the family circle and the tie that binds us together in Christian love. I know You are with me, regardless of where I am or what my mission in life may be. Help me to recognize this fact more and more during these days of separation. Ease any pains of homesickness and distress that may trouble me.

Wherever the path of duty may lead, guide and protect me. Keep me cheerful and contented in doing Your will. Give me a sense of fulfillment as I faithfully serve others in selfless love. Bring me ultimately home to my family in health and happiness. And finally lead us to our heavenly home, where we shall be eternally blessed in Your presence. Then our cup of joy will be full. In Jesus' name I pray. Amen.

When in Danger

I am concerned, dear Lord, for my life and safety. Forgive my anxiety and my little faith, and give me courage to face the dangers and ordeals confronting me. As Your blessed Son knelt in the garden and committed His life and mission for us into Your hands, so I place myself and all things into Your care and keeping.

Almighty Father, I know that Your will is done in all things. Strengthen my faith and trust in Your providential leading. I pray for all my fellowmen who are in any kind of danger, especially for those who do not know Your gracious Word and precious promises. Cause Your kingdom to come to all men, and deliver us all from evil. I am confident of Your constant guidance, help, protection, and deliverance from trouble as I bring this petition in the name of Christ, my Lord and Savior. Amen.

During Illness

Gracious God, help me to accept Your will in my illness. As Your child I believe that You cause all things to work together for my good, both of body and of spirit. But sometimes in the midst of illness and pain I forget or doubt. Forgive my weak faith. When I become impatient, encourage me by Your Word. Despite my worry and suffering, help me by my life to reflect the radiance and confidence of one certain of Your promises of help. Restore me to sound health if it be Your will, and enable me with new vigor and enthusiasm to serve You zealously for many years to come. Give me Your Holy Spirit that I may always witness joyfully to my Christian faith before men, confessing that all life, on earth and in heaven, is a gift from You. O Lord, have mercy. Hear my prayer for Jesus' sake. Amen.

For a Christian Home

Lord God, heavenly Father, continue to bless us as a family, and make our home truly Christlike. Give us the power to overcome temptations, and the wisdom to avoid the frictions that can destroy a family. Preside in our home by setting up Your throne in our hearts and lives. Give us Your Spirit to inspire us to live out our Christian faith in all our family relationships. Strengthen our family ties as we gather regularly about Your Word for devotions and prayer. By Your grace and mercy give us willingness to forgive one another even as we are forgiven for Jesus' sake.

We ask that our home become not merely a place where we gather to eat and to sleep, but truly a Christian home in which we dwell in mutual love and affection. By Your Spirit's influence in our lives make and keep us one happy family, living together in peace and harmony as becomes members of the body of Christ. Grant us the security, love, and joy that we are promised in our Lord Christ. In His name we ask this. Amen.

In a Troubled Home

Heavenly Father, we are in trouble — in deep trouble in our home. By Your grace and mercy in Christ, help us.

We have become so involved with this world, its affairs and attractions, that we have forgotten You. We failed to pray, "Lead us not into temptation," as we ought. Forgive the sins of forgetfulness and ingratitude we committed when we failed to acknowledge Your presence and blessing in our daily lives. Make us realize that we cannot live without You and never can succeed as a family without Your love in our hearts.

Restore peace and harmony among us. Assist us to understand and respect one another. Change us by the power of Your Holy Spirit, and endow us with the mind of Christ. Grant us the grace to forgive and to be patient with all the members of our family. Restore our oneness in Christ. Turn our energies from quarreling among ourselves to serving You and our fellowman. Give us a foretaste of the fellowship and joy we shall have in our home in heaven. In Jesus' name. Amen.

For a Wayward Child

"Why, oh, why?" is the question that plagues us, dear Lord. Why did this happen to our child? Where did we fail? What did we do wrong? Where was our weakness? Wasn't our home life what it should have been? Were we too lax? Or too strict in our discipline? Didn't we reveal the power of Christ's love and forgiveness in our lives, the devotion and concern that Christians owe one another in our family relationships? Lord, have mercy and forgive us our failures and sins. Come to us and abide in our lives with Your love, granting us patience, understanding, and peace in our home.

Give our wayward one the spirit of humility and reconciliation, and lead him to resume his role of a loving and dutiful child in our family. O Lord, by the remembrance of his baptism lead him to return to You, and prompt him to live henceforth in agreement with Your Word and will. Finally, by Your strange but loving guidance, cause this present experience to prove a blessing to all concerned. Hear us, good Lord, for Jesus' sake. Amen.

In a Marriage Crisis

Merciful God and Father, our marriage is at the breaking point. We are unable to communicate with one another. We cannot withstand the inner tensions and the external pressures that tear people apart unless You intervene. Help us, good Lord. Spare us the curse of a broken marriage. Do not permit us to forget Your Word and gracious will for us as husband and wife. Forgive our sins and enable us to overcome disharmony. Remove unkind words from our lips. Help us stop loveless criticism and quarreling. Rule our hearts by Your love. Keep us together and make us whole in Christ.

You are our only hope in life and in death. Give us faith in Your promises, and bolster our trust in Your power and will to heal our marriage breach. Since the future is in Your hands, we ask You to convert our marital troubles into blessings in disguise for us both. Through them lead us to become more appreciative of one another, more understanding and forgiving, until one day as faithful husband and wife we inherit Your promise of eternal peace and joy reserved for us in heaven; for Jesus' sake. Amen.

PERSONAL PRAYERS

For Acceptance of Self

Father, teach me to trust the Spirit You have breathed into me. Give me grace to believe Your Word, by which I am made Your child. Help me to understand that I belong to You, even though I am undeserving of Your love.

Help me to see Your judgment and mercy in the suffering and death and resurrection of my Lord Jesus Christ. Cause me to accept again the new life in Christ which You have given me by faith. Enable me to live without despair and without pride. Lead me to know with joy that You accept me as a whole human being.

Father, teach me one more thing. Show me that in this new life You give I no longer have to build walls of fear to protect myself from others. Help me to live cheerfully and generously, so that others may receive You through Christ's Word and work in me and begin to live in You. Bless me and keep me for Jesus' sake. Amen.

Thanksgiving and Praise

Great and wondrous God, Creator and Keeper of the world, You are so high above and beyond my little thoughts and ways that I cannot by my own reason or strength comprehend the extent and fullness of Your being. With thanks and praise I acknowledge Your majesty and power.

Because in Your steadfast love and mercy You have made Yourself my Father in Jesus Christ and re-created me in the image of His holiness, I cannot by my own reason or strength comprehend the extent and fullness of Your love.

In faith I thank and praise Your grace and mercy. You do so much for me without any merit in me that all I can do is thank and praise Your holy name through Jesus Christ, my Lord. Amen.

Birthday

In the name of the Father and of the Son and of the Holy Spirit I begin another year.

I want to live each day in the clear knowledge that it is Your day.

Keep me active in service to You and my fellowman during this coming year.

Show me Your love and mercy in Christ as You have done in the past.

Give me opportunities to share Christ's love and mercy with others, and give me the strength and the will to do so.

Let my birthday be the reminder of how much I am in debt to You for Your constant care, concern, and love.

Help me to live this year of grace as Your child, O Lord. Amen.

Vocation

Lord of my life, I ask Your blessing on my daily life and especially on my work. My work is good because Your hand is upon it. Do not let me turn my work to selfish purposes. Forgive me when I fail.

Help me to remember that You are still Lord when I feel discouraged and useless or when I am tense and angry. Help me to remember You are still Lord when I am satisfied and pleased with my accomplishments.

Take my work into Your own hands. Give blessing to all I do and say. Use what I accomplish as a blessing to others, for Jesus' sake. Amen.

In Illness (1)

Merciful and healing Lord, for some reason which I do not understand the usual pattern of my daily life has been disrupted. You are asking me to give up the familiar and comfortable routine of my work and to struggle for a while with this unfamiliar and uncomfortable pain.

Lord, sit beside me now and help me to learn the purpose which this illness is to accomplish. Help me to see how much and how often I have relied on my own strength, my own cleverness, my own ability. Forgive my pride that will not let me depend on You.

In my illness help me to see that I am truly well when I remember that I belong to You. If it be Your will, restore me soon to health and a life of active service. Fill me with the life of the Spirit, that in Christ I may be blessed and be a blessing to others.

Hear my prayer in Jesus' name. Amen.

In Illness (2)

Father,
Hear me.
Have mercy.
Help me.
Have mercy.
Heal me
with Your peace.

Father,
I am in Your hands.
Have mercy.
Give peace.
Amen.

Before Surgery

Dear Father in heaven, go with me to surgery. Guide my doctor's hands so that his work may be done skillfully and quickly. As my Great Physician grant that all my trust may be in You and that I may have no fear.

Receive me now as Your forgiven child, and bring me safely through these next hours. In the name and for the sake of Jesus Christ, my Savior. Amen.

After Surgery

Thank You, Lord, my God.

Thank You for the gift of skillful hands and minds which have been used in my behalf.

Thank You for the gift of care, kindly administered through nurses, aids, and orderlies.

Thank You for the gift of medical science that eases my pain and makes me comfortable and helps me recover.

Thank You for Your Son Jesus Christ, who calms my fear and fills me with joy by His presence.

Grant me a speedy recovery if it be Your will. Strengthen me in spirit as well as in body.

Help me to use the days ahead to grow in my trust of Your goodness, through Your Son. Amen.

During Convalescence (1)

Loving Father, I came to You in pain and confusion and fear, and You have brought me out of the deep shadow of death.

I know, Father, that You long to keep me always in Your hands and that You desire I trust You in everything. Keep this lesson fresh in my heart. Let me never forget that even when I am strong I am weak and sinful.

For the sake of Christ Jesus, my Lord and Savior, forgive the doubts and fears that hound me. Do not deal harshly with me. Let me never forget that when I am weak You make me strong by the strength of Your love and mercy in Jesus Christ, my Lord. Amen.

During Convalescence (2)

Thank You, Lord, for the protection, love, and mercy You give me. Teach me to understand that the life You have mended by Your love has experienced the greater miracle of Your healing forgiveness.

Give me grace to accept with gratitude the privilege to return to my family and friends. Receive my thanks that through my illness You have been always at my side as my heavenly Father.

You have delivered me out of the day of trouble. For all Your goodness I shall now glorify Your name through Christ, my Lord. Amen.

At the Approach of Death

Lord Jesus Christ, come now and hear my prayer. Your cross and empty tomb have turned this last, dark, silent moment to a time of light, hope, and everlasting joy. I remember my baptism, when I was received into the kingdom of heaven.

Remember me, Lord, and forgive me once more. Remember me, Lord, and receive me as You promised.

It will be time very soon to leave all those who are dear and familiar to me, and this is hard to do. They have been Your gifts to me, Lord, and I thank You for them. Be with them now.

In the midst of death, tell them, Lord, that we live together in You. Remind them, Lord, to give praise and thanksgiving for the Father's tender and loving mercy. Teach them, Lord, to sing the song of Easter morning.

In the name of the Father and of the Son and of the Holy Spirit. Hallelujah! Amen.

After a Death

Father, Your hand is heavy upon me now. Teach me to understand Your will and Your ways.

Father, I thank You for the blessing that _____ has been to me.

Praise God from whom all blessings flow!

Father, I thank You for the love that has called _____ to Your side and calls me to rejoice.

Praise Him, all creatures here below!

Father, I thank You for the mercy that sent Your own Son into death so that we will never be defeated by death.

Praise Him above, ye heavenly host!

Father, I thank You for the love which through the resurrection of Your Son keeps us alive by Your Spirit even in the midst of death.

Praise Father, Son, and Holy Ghost!

You can take away the heaviness of my sorrow. Fill me with joy and let me share the peace of the undefeated life in Christ with _____ forevermore. Amen.

When Away from Home

Heavenly, watchful Father, as Jesus traveled the roads of Galilee, far from His home, You were with Him. So as I travel and live in places away from my home, keep me in Your presence and hold me close to You.

Keep me from harm and danger, and from temptations which make me forget You and those who love me. Live in me with strength and joy, so that strangers and friends may see in me the blessing of Your presence.

I ask especially for Your strength to support me in the moments of longing and loneliness. Direct these moments away from self-pity and toward a trust in Your care for all of us.

Live also in my home. Watch over my loved ones. Keep us all with the loving benediction of Your fatherly care. So all will be well, and all will be kept together while we are apart. Amen.

In Temptation

Lord Jesus Christ, stay with me.

There is evil around me, and I am so often attentive to it. It is beautiful sometimes, and sensible, and practical, and friendly —or so it seems.

Lord Jesus Christ, stay with me.

There is evil within me, and I am so often attentive to it. I am easily overcome by my own desire to get away from You and be free to have everything I want and to do everything I want.

Lord Jesus Christ, give me the real freedom of Your life in me. By Your victory over temptations make me victorious. By the power of Your love make me strong.

Lord Jesus Christ, without You I will fall. With You I can stand against the enemy. Stay with me. Amen.

In Doubt

Father, You are able to
    create out of nothing.
I confess my heart is
    reduced to nothingness by
    doubts, fears, grief, and
    despair.
I live in the darkness
    of hopelessness.
I confess that the world
    has failed to remove my doubts
    by its rewards and promises
    of material things, by its
    pursuit of pleasure, by its
    worship of science.
Remove the doubts that haunt me,
    that I may know the joy of salvation.
Let me trust Your goodness as Creator,
    Your faithfulness, Your grace,
    and Your forgiveness as Lord of my life;
    through Jesus Christ. Amen.

In Anger

I cannot pretend, Lord.
You know I am angry,
and You know I act like I never knew You.
But You are here.

Hold back my fury with Your love.
Turn me around again,
so that I may be filled with Your love
that won forgiveness for all men.
Enable me to speak forgiveness
in Your name. Amen.

In Loneliness

Father, in the noisy congestion and confusion of my life I am standing by myself. Somehow I have lost contact with others. Somehow I no longer feel related to others. I am lonely. I cannot live this way, Lord.

Draw me back into the circle of friends. In mercy send me to someone who can offer Your love. Help me to discover again the power of Your love for restoring unity and fellowship with others.

As You promise to be with me always in Christ my Lord, help me to live always for others, in love for Him who overcame loneliness for me. Amen.

For Companionship

Heavenly Father, You have created us for companionship and have re-created us for fellowship in our Lord Jesus Christ. I confess I often disrupt fellowship by thoughtlessness and selfishness.

I pray for forgiveness. Destroy in me the vanity that keeps me from liking others. Help me overcome the timidity that makes me fearful of others. Keep me from the urge to take advantage of others, but discourage in me the feeling that I cannot call on others.

Help me to find friendship among those who know the constant love and mercy of Your Son. Enable me to choose good and loyal friends. Enable me to be kind, generous, and forgiving.

I pray in the name of Jesus, who brought me into the fellowship of the church. Amen.

For Integrity

Lord God, You know what I am. Give me the courage to face the truth about myself, to recognize my failures, to know my inadequacies, to understand my weaknesses.

Keep me from pride and deceit. Do not permit me to make my life counterfeit or to hide behind some cheap pretense.

In the crucified Christ let me see the depth of my sin, the grossness of my selfishness, and the judgment of death I deserve. In the risen Christ let me see the new life You give me by Your grace, experiencing the deliverance from my old self and the freedom to live for You. With the mind of Christ ruling me, let me be honest with You, with myself, and with all men.

In the name of Christ I pray. Amen.

For Diligence

Heavenly Father, Creator of all good things and Redeemer of the world, give me Your Spirit that I may be a good and faithful steward. Forgive me when I leave matters undone, fail to begin what I should, neglect my talents, and misuse my gifts. Help me to do the difficult and bitter tasks as well as the pleasant and joyful duties. Make me diligent in using my energies to full capacity. Help me to be zealous in all my work. Give me ambition for unselfish service. Prompt me to serve You and those around me for Your sake. Bless me with the joy of an unworthy steward who has been made worthy through the merits of Jesus Christ, my Savior. Amen.

For Humility

O righteous and gracious Father, because You sent Your Son in the form of a humble servant, create in me the mind of Christ that I may be Your servant. Destroy in me false humility that is really pride, false pride that is really fear, and false hopes that will not face reality.

Expose the shabbiness, phoniness, and emptiness of my pretenses and dreams. In Christ accept me as I am and give to me the blessing of His innocence. By His dying and rising again, permit me to rise out of the death of pride to new life in humility. So will I be blessed through Him whom You exalted to be my Lord. Amen.

For Joy

Dear God, in You I must live if I am to be alive. I confess I am filled with sadness. I have lost the sense of joy. I have become sick of today, and I do not care about tomorrow. I feel the hours drag on.

God, my Father, release me from this emptiness. In the midst of this oppressive weakness, restore to me the joy of Your salvation. Remind me of the cross on which Your Son bore the guilt of my sin. Remind me of the empty tomb by which He gained for me the freedom to live.

Help me to live in the joy of my freedom. Prepare me to meet every new day with joy. Prepare me to accept new tasks with joy. Prepare me to live in the midst of the terrors of this world with joy and confidence.

Thank You, God my Father, for the joy and peace that revive me and restore me to life. Amen.

For Patient Endurance

Gracious God, I am troubled and disheartened. Time is a heavy burden for me. I grow weary, discouraged, and fearful because of my problems. Yet I know You can rescue me from my confusion. You set the stars to move in precise rhythm, and You can bring order to my affairs. To You a thousand years are but a day, and You can give me the patience to live today as a day of grace. To You one day can be as a thousand years, and You can help me to live today with the hope and patience of eternity.

In Jesus Christ, Your Son, You have begun the new age of life and immortality. In Him give me courage and strength. Amen.

For Wisdom and Maturity

Lord God, You revealed in Jesus Christ that Your foolishness exceeds the wisdom of men, and Your weakness is greater than their strength. Give me the grace and wisdom to understand that in Your gentleness there is power, in Your kindness there is might, in Your forgiveness there is life. Keep me from the folly of relying on my own power or my own purpose. Help me to see that wisdom is born and grows to maturity through faith in Christ. Grant me confidence in Your mercy and hope in Your promises.

I pray in the name of Him who is Wisdom. Amen.

For the Ability to Forgive

Lord Jesus Christ,
You have taught me to pray:
>"Forgive us our trespasses as we
>forgive those who trespass against us."

In Your name
>*I* am to repair the breach;
>*I* am to mend the broken;
>*I* am to welcome back the
>>wanderer who returns.

Lord Jesus Christ,
>help me to understand
>that this power is Your power,
>to be used for the sake of those
>for whom You died.

Help me to understand
>that I cannot turn away from any
>who ask for forgiveness or need
>my forgiveness.

Help me to overcome
>any hindrance that would keep me
>from sharing the fullness and the
>power of Your saving and forgiving
>grace.

I ask it in the power of Your name. Amen.

For Acceptance of Others

Forgive me, Father, for my unwillingness to share Your gift of life with others.

My eyesight is so often faulty. I do not see others as You see them. I judge by my own standards and reject those who do not measure up.

My hearing is faulty, too. I listen to those who can help me, but do not hear those who need me.

Father, You see us all through the eyes of Jesus Christ and accept us for His sake. You hear us and know that we need Your forgiveness and mercy.

Even so, Father, teach me Your way of seeing and hearing Your people in whatever circumstance I find them. Give me a full measure of understanding and compassion, so that my actions and words will reflect the fatherly love and mercy You have given me. Amen.

For Personal Dedication

Lord of my life, I know that my life is not my own. By Your death and resurrection You made me Your own. Help me to live under Your direction, always ready to hear the call, "Follow Me"; always aware of Your presence; always knowing that I have received the gift of Your Spirit; always living so that others may receive Your love and mercy through me.

It is not easy to ask for these things, Lord, because I know I have much to give up. I can no longer pretend that my life is my own. My prayer is my surrender to Your care and direction. I want to follow, Lord, but it is very hard. I will get very tired. I will make selfish mistakes. I will fail time and again. I will fall.

Show me again that there is love and forgiveness and mercy in Your hand. Use me in spite of my reluctance, doubt, and disobedience.

Pour into me Your good Spirit, so that I am not afraid to follow and fall and follow again. Amen.